THE Ernie Kovacs PHILE

RCA

by David G. Walley

B O L D E R

All of the material quoted in THE ERNIE KOVACS PHILE is reprinted with permission from the Ernie Kovacs Estate, except for the following: Portions of *Stinky Water Notes* reprinted with permission from *The Trentonian*, Trenton, NJ. *ZOOMAR*, copyright © 1957 by Ernie Kovacs. Reprinted by permission of Doubleday & Co., Inc. Special thanks to *MAD MAGAZINE* for permission to reprint issue #38,pp.19,31 from "Strangely Believe It" (artist W. Wood), back cover illust: "Barker 61 Pen" (artist Kelly Freas) copyright © 1958 by E.C. Publications, Inc. "Gringo" pps56-57 (artist W. Elder) from *MAD FOR KEEPS* copyright © 1956 by E.C. Publications, Inc. Published by Crown Publishers, 1958. **PHOTO CREDITS:** All of the photos contained in THE ERNIE KOVACS PHILE are the property of Robert A. Kemp, except for the following: photo #1,5,19,20,21,22, and 24 reprinted with permission from The Memory Shop, 109, East 12 Street, NYC. The author's photo is reprinted with permission from Julie Heifitz.

Published by Bolder Books, a division of
Hampstead Hall Press, Ltd., 10 East 40 Street, New York, NY 10016.
Published originally in hardcover by Drake Publishers, Inc., under the title: *Nothing In Moderation*.

ISBN: 0-918282-06-3
LIBRARY OF CONGRESS CATALOG CARD NUMBER: 78-64637

Cover design by Peter Davis.

First Printing

Printed in the USA

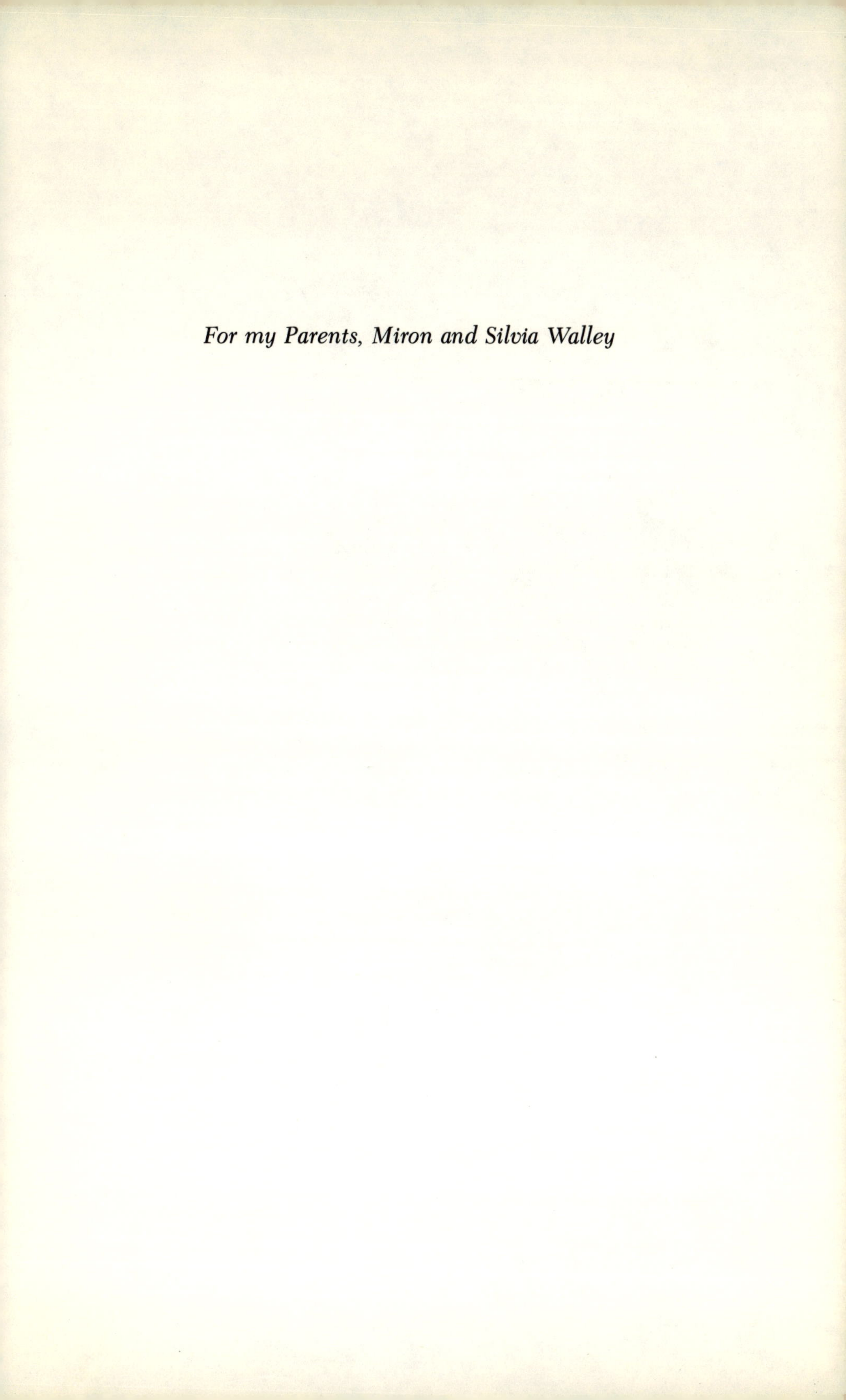

For my Parents, Miron and Silvia Walley

1. The Opening Credits *9*
2. Stinky Water Notes *30*
3. Dead Lion For Breakfast *58*
4. Admit One Passing Stranger *80*
5. Miklos Molnar Meets Motzah Hepplewhite *120*
6. Eugene in Tinseltown *145*
7. It's Been Real *203*

APPENDICES

A. Kovacs On Music *219*

B. Jealousy — a memo *225*

C. Prop List — 12/30/52 *232*

D TV, Radio, and Filmography *235*

This is really a television script and not for radio at all. But as you will see, the prospects of having it produced aren't very good. At the risk of seeming naive, I'll state that there is a slight problem of casting. You see, in the play I have definite views as to who should play each part. The play is about movie stars, and in the play I want Spencer Tracy to play a part called Marlon Brando. Marlon Brando to play a character called Walter Pidgeon, who, in turn, plays Cary Grant. And then for a complete circle, Cary Grant plays Spencer Tracy. In fact, there's only one part in the whole play that doesn't present a casting problem. That's the part of Buzz Benson, a young television producer. The play is rather a play within a play. It begins, simply enough, at MGM *studios in Buzz Benson's plush office. Everyone is there. Buzz speaks,*

"Gentlemen," he says, "what we got here is something. Really big." The movie stars murmur. Marlon Brando, who is really Spencer Tracy, replies, "I don't like it." He then undoes his shirt, removes a glove from his pocket, puts the glove on, and scratches his stomach with his other hand. Walter Pidgeon, who is Marlon Brando, says, "It smacks of deceit." Now Cary Grant, played by Spencer Tracy, agrees with him. The young director is stymied. Cary Grant/Spencer Tracy in real life then asks, "Who am I?" Marlon replies that, "If ya don't know, how d'ya expect . . . " Walter Pidgeon says, "Well done, Marlon." He then shakes the real Marlon Brando's hand, then, embarrassed by his mistake, he crosses quickly to Spencer Tracy and says the line again, "Well done, Marlon." Now everybody laughs a little, but not enough to destroy empathy. Of course, this is easier to understand if you can picture it. You see, all these stars are playing other big stars. What I'm trying to do in the play is to destroy type casting — and I think I've done it.

— A one-page "possibility" by Ernie Kovacs called
TYPE CASTING

It is Saturday, January 13, 1962, in Beverly Hills, on a typical Southern California winter's night. There is mist in the air; a fine rain is falling. Off the intersection of Wilshire Boulevard and Beverly Glen, a christening party is in progress in the apartment of Billy Wilder, the director. It could as easily be a gathering in West Covina or Hightstown, New Jersey, but here Milton Berle is being feted on the occasion of his newest son Michael, and all his Hollywood friends have come to wish him well: Dean Martin and Jeanie, his wife at the time; Yves Montand; Lucille Ball and her new husband, Gary Morton; Jack Lemmon; director Richard Quine; and many others. This party has been going on for years at different houses in this rarified community of stars, agents, producers, and directors. Nothing unusual here. They chit-chat, drink their drinks, and consume the catered Chassen's chili.

Also in attendance is Ernie Kovacs, a large-framed, cigar-smoking, television comedian who's been in Hollywood for the past five years, pursuing a career in film. He's already done eight films; his newest, *Sail a Crooked Ship,* in which he plays a tippling, bumbling captain of a hijacked cargo ship, is about to be released. For the past three or four days, he has been on a treadmill between the shooting of a television pilot for Screen Gems, a comedy Western called *A Pony for Chris,* and working on his seventh television special for Dutch Masters cigars, which he has been directing, writing, and editing. He is tired, his bushy black eyebrows are weather-beaten. His friends, those members of the "Rat Pack," Jack Lemmon, Frank Sinatra, Dean Martin, and Joey Bishop, who've played many a hand of gin and stud poker in Ernie's outrageously opulent armorial den, are concerned about his health.

But tonight Kovacs seems to be his old wise-cracking self as he regales his friends with tales of shooting a movie bare-chested in Griffith Park. He tells Jeanie Martin that he's going to live forever. How? "All it takes is three steam baths a day, lots of good brandy, about twenty cigars, and work all night." If he sleeps at all, he averages less than three hours a night. He is infamous, king of the clubhouse, for hosting marathon poker and gin parties in his steam room. Jeanie is concerned about the effect of those steam baths on his heart. "Look, kid," he says, "this is the only life I've got and I want to live it the way I like! If I go, I want it to be my way. Besides, those steam baths don't hurt me; I can go all the time, all day and night." He neglects to mention he's been living like this for 20 of his 42 years. He will be 43 in a week.

Kovacs has been a Puck figure ever since he came to Hollywood. In January of 1957, he did a television special, a show without dialogue but with plenty of sight gags and revolutionary camera tricks. Columbia Pictures offered him a large five-figure contract as a result. Of late, he'd been negotiating with Alec Guinness for a production deal and Kovacs was pleased with himself. For the first time since he'd been here, he would have a chance to do what *he* wanted even though his Columbia deal did not allow him to pick his own scripts. In this new deal he would be able to exercise his creative freedom in a medium that had fascinated him for a long time.

The party ambles along until about one o'clock and then Ernie decides to call it quits. He's going to PJ's, one of his haunts on Santa Monica and Crescent Heights Boulevards in Hollywood, to meet a friend for a nightcap. The white Rolls that brought him to the party is outside along with the white Corvair station wagon Edie had driven down from the house. It's nasty outside and he's tired, so he decides to take the station wagon. He tells his wife to drive the "other heap" home.

On the way out, he passes Yves Montand and asks him if he needs a lift to his hotel. "No," Montand says. He's already promised Milton and Ruth Berle he'll ride with them, thanks just the same. Ernie waves good-bye and jumps into his car, sinking heavily into the cushions — the seatbelt unfastened as he tools down Beverly Glen.

The fine winter drizzle has made the roadway slick, water vapor mixing with the exhaust fumes on the heavily traveled road. The man with the big cigar and the big hands driving the cheaply constructed, unstable, rear-engine Corvair station wagon is really too bushed to concentrate on his driving. It's a familiar enough route from Wilder's to PJ's anyway — the car just drives itself, though a little too fast for the present conditions. What the hell! Ernie really isn't thinking about the road or his driving. He owes the government a cool $400,000 which, if he can help it, they'll never see. They're about to tag the furniture and he has just signed over $20,000 in government bonds that he'd been saving for the children. Then there are those IOU's that he's floated all over town, incurred in the course of a run-in with Lady Luck, but he's sure the cards will change for him if he keeps at it . . . just one more hand. He's driving now through the Los Angeles Country Club grounds on the way to Santa Monica Boulevard.

Time for a smoke, the twentieth or twenty-first of the day. He extracts from his jacket pocket another of those foot-long Havana cigar specials, which are his trademark, his obsession, and his pleasure. They line his pocket like bandoliers of ammunition. Fumbling for a kitchen match, he attempts to strike it with his fingernail, a habit he picked up long ago ("ya see, the cigar's got to be caressed by the flame, and lighters ruin the taste."). In that split second, as his car is approaching the intersection, the wheels snag the concrete triangle that meet at the junction of Beverly Glen and Santa Monica Boulevard. His fatigue-ridden senses overcompensate in braking. Like a slow-motion movie, in a deathly parabola, the vehicle starts to skid to the right. His hands clutch the wheel in a frantic effort to steer through what will undoubtedly be a messy, final event. Both of his hands are on the wheel, the unlit cigar clasped between the first and second fingers of his right hand.

The white Corvair station wagon with its revolutionary rear-engine displacement smashes broadside into the telephone poles lining the road. Ernie is thrown to the other side of the front seat, buffeted by the force of the driver's door striking the poles. The passenger door springs open from the concussion, as Ernie, in shock with cigar still in hand, attempts to extricate himself from the twisted metal heap, ignorant of the hairline fracture he's sustained when his head hit the steering wheel. In a last convulsive motion, he manages to reach over the front seat in a futile crawl, and dies. The unlit cigar drops from his hand, resting a few feet from his body, just out of reach of his outstretched right arm.

• • •

Television in the late Forties and Fifties was a live medium and essentially experimental. The mistakes made were the mistakes the viewer saw. Part of the fun of Kovacs was the mistakes. Television of the Fifties, where the newscasts were gray and the comedy was camp, was a collection of Borscht Belt routines with stars like the glitter drag queen Milton Berle. Kovacs was not a Milton Berle, a George Gobel, a Red Skelton, or a Buster Keaton. But Kovacs had the wistful innocence of Chaplin and the off-color ad-lib wit of Groucho Marx. His scripts, if there was a script at all, were never sacred. He wrote 9/10 of his own material. "Every idea I ever had is based on the fact that it's 2:30 and there's a production meeting at 3:00." Kovacs created most of his comedy in the heat of the moment when the little red light of Camera One was on. Rather than scripts, he preferred visions: an automated office where the water cooler gurgled and the file cabinets sang like trumpets, a hand came out of a bathtub to scrub the back of a pretty girl, or the White Rock Girl taking a bath in the effervescent brook of ginger-ale-land.

Born with a cigar in his mouth and a deck of cards in his hands, Kovacs regularly lanced the banal with his sardonic wit. He was especially fond of poking fun at the bread-and-circus syndrome of daytime television quiz shows. In "I've Got a Hush-Hush" the guest whispered his secret in the moderator's ear with the viewing audience also in on the fun. However, in Ernie's version, the guest whispered his secret and then left. Neither the audience nor the panelists ever found out what the "hush-hush" was. Blackout.

Another game he played a few times called "Whom Done It?" where a panelist and possibly the home viewing audience was supposed to guess what crime a contestant had committed — but nothing was ever that simple — especially the rules:

If our astute panel members fail to guess whom done it, the contestant will receive many wonderful prizes, unless he has used a sentence in answering the questions which ends with a preposition, in which case he not only will not receive any prizes, but must contribute equal and same prizes to each of the panelists, with one exception.

Should one of the panelists use a question containing a double negative, he or she will have to change clothes with someone in the audience and will then lose his turn on the panel for the remainder of that round. Unless the person with whom he changes clothing is seated in the third seat of the fourth row, in which case, it will be the person in the audience who will change clothes with the losing panelist. There now — I think all of the rules are clear and here's how we play "Whom Done It?"

To today's sophisticated viewers, these rules sound ridiculous but "Whom Done It?" was no sillier than any number of shows that were appearing at the dawn of daytime television. TV in the Fifties, as it is to a larger degree today, was a selling medium for soap, suppositories, and status — a medium of control with hour upon hour of smiling emcees exploiting human misery and greed. Kovacs, for all his levity and jokes about the stupidity of television, was deeply committed to making it into an adult medium instead of a haven for twelve-year-old minds.

Near the height of his popularity, Kovacs wrote a *Life* magazine cover story on the subject, stating "The television audience of today is a sophisticated, alert, discriminating audience, quick to reject the inadequate. The picture of a nationwide audience holding its sides in ecstatic empathy as a smiling young man runs up and down the aisles kissing old ladies and handing out orchids to grandmothers is one that has been removed to the attic, along with the kinescopes of those programs." He believed that in the end it was the networks that would have to bend, "The networks, desiring to maintain and create further programming accomplishments, will have to compromise their cost-accounting system."

In the end, it was the same cost-accounting system that contributed to Ernie's financial ruin. When he was producing his own television specials, the omniscient studio accountant understood little of Ernie's methods of theater and even less of television production. Thus, the estimated cost of Ernie's first Dutch Masters special for April, 1961, was $11,174. The actual costs by showtime became $25,185. Budgeted rehearsal time was 12 hours on paper, but actually turned out to be more like 25 hours. The final tag included an additional $5,000 for production penalties as well as double and triple overtime for the crews, since Ernie believed in continuity of action. In real terms, that meant long hauls of 24 to 30 hours straight. There were rumors around the ABC television lot that many of Ernie's technicians were driving around in Cadillacs due to Ernie's spend-it-like-water theories of labor.

Ernie created a stableful of characters: the infamous Percy Dovetonsils; the inscrutable Charlie Clod, Charlie Chan's left-handed cousin; Irving Wong, the Chinese song-plugger; and Wolfgang Sauerbraten, the all-night German disk jockey, a distinguished gray-maned gentle gentleman with lederhosen and an atrocious Hollywood-German accent:

Guttenack, klina fraulines, fraus, und herrs . . . dine disk chockey, Wolfgang Sauerbraten moosiks du liebe . . . klina liebshan, dise nacht we blay zom heis moosiks let ein spreighen de newest b-bopper . . . du dist the moch greunadawn veather . . . spreighen enima lina b-bopper ish der ben cool dis nacht un crazy en morgen — eh? Ich weiss nich was is sogen . . . unlaben, leichen, en spreichet ein commercial . . . .

closing with, of course, a word from the sponsor:

Ach, sich shoen blamieren. Ich musten eilen. Es suspat. Ich haben hayben musten spreichen gutton nachte. Un remindun, davega storen, feer dreis 42 strasse, binb bomb tables, catcher mitts und hockey shticks . . . gutten nachte aus Wolfgang Sauerbraten, du all nachen disk chockey.

All pure ad lib, Kovacs just got into costume and into character on camera. A born mimic, he made any accent (including his ancestral Hungarian) his own, and used it with mirthful intent as he did in the commercial for Colonel Janos Kentucky Fried Paprikas. Only in the world of Ernie Kovacs could there be such a creature as a Kentucky Hungarian spieling the following shtick:

Us Kentucky Hungarians know yo' folks is sick of a-fussin' ovah youah paprikas. So us Kentucky Hungarians figgered yo' like to know whuts on the inside . . .
(Close up of soup spoon with one Ping-Pong ball in it)
A nice round potato, home grown to puffection on a Kentucky lathe . . .
(Cross dissolve to c.u. of toothpick with three peas stuck on it)

Wolfgang Sauerbraten

Three rich, green peas grown in dark brown Budapest gravy and deep-fat-fried to puffect excellence . . . and the whole mess of rich, deep-lovin' goodness is fricasseed fo'elebem hours . . .

(Cross dissolve to c.u. of bottle labeled "Kentucky Budapest Bourbon")

. . . in solid 180 proof Kentucky Budapest Bourbon. So, as ol' Sam Janos used to say, "An' remembah — Make sure it's Janos."

And, of course, there were his cheapo epic films, parodies of late-night television reruns — cheap because during much of the time in his early days, he never had a budget for the props he needed. Hence the silent-movie treatment. A roller jerkily unfolds the credits:

IVBAN TROO DE MILL
PRESENTS
A TALE OF ESPIONAGE
Undercover Goings on in a Restaurant
Coldcuts of Steel in Hotbeds of Spies

RANSACKED RADAR!
HIJACKED HYDROGEN!
PILFERED PEROXIDE!
BOY!

See Sneaky Spies at Work
See Uncle Sam Strike Back
See the Charge of Wild Bull Elephants
SWOLLEN RIVERS
The Dynamiting of Hoover Dam (NARTB)
WITH A CAST OF A FEW!
See Headless Heroines

ON THESTRETCHOMATICSCREEN!
WITH SCHIZOPHRENICSOUND!
IN GLORIOUS GRAYS AND BLACKS!

As Told to Ivban Troo De Mill by
A Former Irish Spy!

WE ARE INDEBTED TO THE F.B.I. FOR THE LOAN OF THEIR TYPEWRITER WITHOUT WHICH THIS SCRIPT WOULD NOT HAVE BEEN POSSIBLE

THE CAST IN THE ODOR OF THEIR APPEARANCE

ARCHDUKE O'TOOLE .... Manny Shevitz
CAROUSEL TICKET COLLECTOR ....
Bushmaster Kreel
LADY PAMELA MAINWARING ....
Bessie Lou Cosnowski
THE THE HOODED STRANGER Listerine Goldfarb
USED GONDOLA SALESMAN ...... Cordella Pfunf
ELDERLEY MAN .... "Whitey" Grootz
THE CHINESE COOK .... Sir Bradford Shultz

• • •

And Introducing Moisch!

Just as in silent movies, typed cue cards conveyed to the actors whatever cheapo action was occurring. In keeping with the loose nature of an Ivban Troo De Mill production, the cue card could be fawled — er, flawed:

MEANWHILE . . . BACK AT TRADER LOUIE'S, THE HOODED STRANGER WAS APPRIE . . . APPREHENSN . . . NERVOUS.

Since nothing was ever easy in Kovacsland, the silent-movie endings were slightly deranged parodies sometimes combined with Gilbert-and-Sullivan-like cases of mistaken identity (as if anyone knew what was going to happen anyway), which produced a dènouement remotely like this for the aforementioned spectacular:

DIALOGUE: *Ah hah! I have caught you, Spy No. 2*

action: Sandy [Stewart, a Kovacs regular in 1953] whips off disguise . . . shows badge on chest . . . speaks

DIALOGUE: *No, I am a female United States Deputy Marshal . . . here is your spy.*

action: Sandy points to Andy [McKay, another Kovacs regular] . . . Andy whips off disguise . . . has similar star . . . speaks

DIALOGUE: *Oh no, likewise, I am a United States Deputy Marshal . . . then . . . Trader Louie's son must be the spy!*

action: all point to Trigger Lund . . . he rips off disguise . . . speaks

DIALOGUE: *Au contraire, fellow United States Deputy Marshals, I too am a United States Deputy Marshal . . .*

action: Ko hits self on head . . . speaks

DIALOGUE: *And we have been following each other for eleven years for nothing!*

action: all begin to choke each other.

THIS FILM WAS ACTUALLY FILMED IN A RESTAURANT ONCE OWNED BY A MAN WHOSE NEIGHBOR WAS A UNITED STATES DEPUTY MARSHAL.

The viewers in Kovacsland were used to this. They expected it. What other show would allow it? What other network? What would an advertisement for Harmon Guggenflekker's Quick Frozen Noodnicks be like? Or Lost Beer? Kovacs's shows were possibly the only ones on television where absolutely no one took anything seriously. Like the "Uncle Gruesome Puppet Show," which sometimes appeared — *sometimes.* Uncle Gruesome was a nice old man who told horrid fairy tales for horrid little boys and girls:

Well . . . here we are again boys and girls . . . you remember last week we left our story in the old moldy cave in the haunted mountain. The three-eyed gargoyle had just made a big pot of dead-bat stew, when someone knocked at the door with a human hip bone. Well, boys and girls, the gargoyle's two-headed pet pussycat meowed twice, once for each child. The rotting door burst open and twelve crazy elephants with green trunks and bloody fangs ran into the kitchen.
(Gruesome looks in opposite direction of cue cards hastily)
Whoops, here comes that old grouch again, time to go, but remember, Auntie Gruesome will be back next Tuesday — brought to you by that wonderful breakfast food that is partially shot from guns, Hot Noodnicks!

Ernie's brand of humor was to go to any lengths to get a laugh. Some of his friends thought this was his weakness. "Better writers, more editing," they thought. But Ernie never used his writers that much. When he arrived in Hollywood in 1957, he came in contact with his comedic peers for the first time. He was good friends with all the vaudeville refugees, especially Groucho Marx, though Ernie's form of humor often eluded them. The inscrutable Jack Benny said to Ernie during a dressing-room conversation, "I don't know what it is about you. I watch, I listen, I laugh."

Ernie had almost no imitators, being one of the few performers whose off-camera personality was the same as his on-camera one. And he certainly had style! He spent an estimated $13,000 per year on special Havana cigars, and

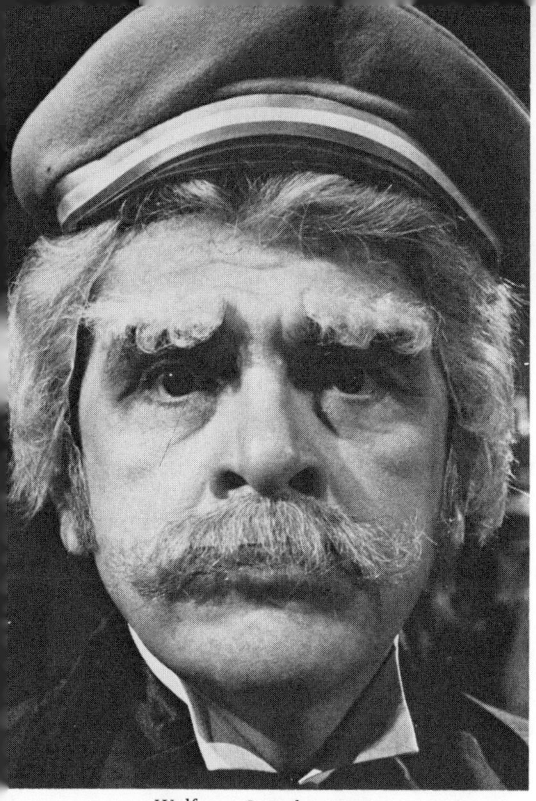
Wolfgang Sauerbraten

A tight spot for a good cigar.

Charlie Clod, private eye

Miklos Molnar

he offered you one almost as soon as he met you. He was the type of man who, if he liked you, wanted to include you in all his activities — a trip to the poker table or the steam room. And if Ernie was associated with cigars throughout his lifetime, he was certainly also associated with cards, which he played with a passion bordering on mania. He was an enthusiastic gambler, though at times unlucky. The type of player who would beat you to death with money. If his bluff failed, he'd say, "Gee, too bad... I thought I had you there." Occasionally he'd win big, like $48,000 in one Hollywood poker game, by pulling two cards to an inside straight. That one was pure luck, but he lost much more than he could ever win. He was such an obsessive gambler that he'd call his friends up in the middle of the night, "Come on down, we need a fourth." and you'd gladly go.

Kovacs lived magnificently, splendidly. The best of everything: big cars with telephones in the back ("I'm approaching Beverly Glen, dear, make sure the martinis are iced"). He was a regular at the Stork Club and Sardi's in New York. Once he ran up a $7,000 tab at Sardi's and when he was asked why he continued to patronize the restaurant, he characteristically replied, "Look if I don't keep coming here, they're going to ask me for the money." He lived for the moment.

This was a fact of his life. He spent water like money — er, money like water. But that wasn't funny really; it was one of the unfunniest threads of Kovacs's life. He'd joke about it, saying to his friends "There's nothing that $80,000 couldn't cure." He couldn't resist the grand gesture. And when he got to Hollywood, which was already filled with big spenders and big tippers, Ernie just couldn't stand to be outdone. He was famous for picking up checks. He was also famous back in his hometown of Trenton, New Jersey, for being the easiest touch in town.

People would line up for blocks just to ask Ernie for money.

Money was a tool, a kick, a gesture — it didn't mean anything. It was fun. He earned it, dammit, he'd spend it. Only Kovacs would have a wine cellar built into his basement with a phony Jack Benny-type combination lock and thick heavy bolts. Only Ernie would wire the special-effects department at ABC to spray fake cobwebs on the bottles. What else was money good for anyway? Either you spent it quick or the government spent it for you on some war or pork-barrel scheme.

Once Ernie came to New York to do a guest spot with his family — his wife Edie and children, Kippie and Bette, plus a maid. He rented a suite of rooms at the Plaza — with room service included, natch. Along about the end of the first week, Ernie discovered that his fee for doing the show would be considerably less than the hotel bill. Ernie put his foot down: he decreed, after much thought, that the whole brood would have to take meals at stated times. At least that would cut down on the room service.

Hollywood seemed to change him — slightly. His cronies may have been Jack Lemmon, Billy Wilder, Tony Curtis, or Edward G. Robinson, but he still had time for his crews — his partners in crime. One of the most unusual aspects of Ernie's lifestyle was his ability to communicate with everyone. In Hollywood the stars rarely if ever condescend to mingle socially with the technicians — the ciphers who do the dirty work. Next to writers, they were the lowest on the social scale. Ernie encouraged the technicians to be as creative as possible on the set and off, to visit his home and try their luck at cards (if they had any money), or just to hang out.

One cameraman, Bob Kemp, who was also Ernie's staff photographer for *Take a Good Look,* an off-the-wall quiz program, brought by some photos one afternoon. Ernie asked him in for a drink.

"Vodka and — " Bob hesitated for a moment.

"You like vodka," said Kovacs. "Just a sec." He opened the freezer in his den and extracted a hoary glass and a bottle of liquid potato. He poured a healthy shot into the glass and said, "Drink this."

Bob was a little surprised and hesitated, taking a small pull.

"No," said Kovacs jovially. "Pour it right down," and he helped Bob pour it right down, setting the poor man on fire. Not content with one, Ernie insisted on a refill, pouring himself one in the process. Within an hour's time they'd killed half the bottle just for the hell of it, because it was there to be drunk and enjoyed.

Kovacs was a walking paradox: he was super machismo, prone to swear with love and determination, but was also gentle, kind, and sensitive. For all his openness, he was an elusive figure — a man of a thousand faces and places.

He came to Hollywood expecting to be received on the strength of his television work, to be allowed to innovate as he'd done on television and radio for the past 17 years in Philadelphia and New York but he discovered the agony of working within a system where the creative urge was regimented by the enforced segregation of writers, producers, and directors mired by agents of all kinds. In Hollywood, if you were type-cast for a role, you were stuck with it.

So Ernie became THE CAPTAIN for Hollywood, and ever after, the comedic para-military villain: Captain Lock in *Operation Madball,* Captain Sègurra in *Our Man in Havana,* Captain Stark in *Wake Me When It's Over,* and The Captain in *Sail'a Crooked Ship.* At one point, Ernie took out an ad in *Hollywood Variety.* "No more #/+#

Captains," it read. Edd Henry, his movie agent from MCA, tried to explain. "I argued the point with Ernie that he wouldn't be considered a star because we had the 'handsome-good-looking,' male lead type — which he wasn't. It was always my feeling that Ernie was a personality, rather than a romantic type. In Hollywood, if you wanted a romantic image, you had to carry the picture, and if the picture was a failure, you were a failure." You are what you project.

Kovacs was an American original who possessed a cock-eyed vision of the world. On January 19, 1957, Kovacs thrilled NBC television audiences with an unexpected half-hour show, a filler for Jerry Lewis. Hired at the last minute, Kovacs, instead of playing it safe, thought to innovate television by presenting an entirely silent, no-dialogue show. The major portion concerned the trials and tribulations of Eugene, a schnook dressed in a Norfolk jacket, who wandered into a stuffy men's club. Eugene was Everyman, a victim of society who always kept his good nature in spite of circumstances beyond his control: His shoes squeaked when he walked, his celery stalks sounded like splitting trees, his coffee poured at a 15-degree angle into his cup, and his olives snare-drummed down the dining-room table.

Eugene, in many ways, was the inverted Kovacs, his foil. If any of Ernie's characterizations was closest to him and most beloved by his fans, it was Eugene with his sense of wonder and innocence in the face of civilized barbarities.

Possibly Ernie would have enjoyed the type of epic where the scantily clad maidens throw rose petals in front of his sedan chair, where the valet in woven-gold toga carries a golf bag filled with cigars, where the Jack Daniels or Wild Turkey on ice is held aloft as he is marched majestically toward the golden sunset. He also might have opened this book like this:

El Captain

FULL LENGTH — *of two apes . . . one sitting in a chair, cigar in mouth with derby, white breakaway vase in hand . . . the other has on a black beret and is seated at a typewriter . . . obviously he is writing something about the other ape.*

SOUND: *electric typewriter*

TITLES ROLL — *while on titles, apes move to another spot . . . the ape at the typewriter is surrounded by ticker tape up to his waist . . . positions are unchanged.*

BACK TO APES — *writer ape spreads arms in dismay, the other ape with the cigar and derby hits writer ape on the head with the vase . . . writer ape whips out submachine gun and riddles other ape . . . Note: no one falls down . . . both stare at viewer . . . .*

We instinctively dislike a tall, heavy man with a mustache. This description applies most specifically to us. When we see us approaching in a mirror, until we recognize the face, we get our dander up. When we see who it is it's worse.

Kovacs on Kovacs in *The Trentonian*

The student director of Trenton High's 1936 production of Gilbert and Sullivan's *HMS Pinafore* is frazzled on account of a clown in the chorus, an ex-preppy named Ernie Kovacs. Not only are his imitations of the director's mannerisms and speech patterns devastatingly accurate, they are undermining his authority! In desperation he calls in the chairman of the drama department, Van Kirk, a man so imposing and theatrical that he can make the Yellow Pages sound like *Hamlet*.

While the young apprentice is out, the chorus relaxes. When the door opens and Van appears with his assistant, there is silence. With a slow, measured tread, Van stalks over to Kovacs as the chorus parts. He halts before the offender and, taking him by the lapels, pulls him down to eye level, questioning him in a low voice so as not to cause further disturbance. "Do you like being in the show?"

"Yes," Kovacs replies in a similarly low tone.

"Are you sure?" reiterates Van.

"Remember — one more word and you're out!"

Thereafter Kovacs does as he's told. The rehearsal is saved and the show is a success.

This young troublemaker had already been through an unsettled childhood before locking horns with the imperious Kirk. The youngest of the Kovacs brood next to brother Tom, Ernie was born on January 19, 1919. Both his parents were strong-willed. Andrew, his father, a heavy-set, boisterous man known as a lady-killer around town, had been a foot patrolman on the Trenton police force, a failed bootlegger, and the proprietor of a small restaurant in town. His idea of a good time was to hire an organ grinder to play on the police chief's lawn at 3 A.M. A tough man, he had immigrated from Hungary at 13. Mary, Ernie's mother, a gifted seamstress, was a handsome woman with a rich laugh. She was fiercely proud of her youngest and constantly at odds with her husband. (Ernie and his brother became experts at disappearing into the woodwork when the grownups were having a go at each other.) As a child, Ernie's favorite trick was to draw footprints all over his bedroom ceiling leading out the window to freedom.

Growing up on Clinton Street on the less prosperous southside of Trenton, Ernie was an unwilling victim of his mother's love. Her doting fingers once made him a marvelous black-velvet Lord Fauntleroy suit at which the neighborhood youths took umbrage. In Ernie's words, "It was like walking around with a sign that said 'kick me.' I would come running home with ten guys chasing me. To make up for it, I had to play on three different baseball teams." Besides her tendency to dress her son like a dandy, Mary also fed him to death. "My mother was one of those parents who thinks a child isn't healthy unless he's buttered in fat. For a long time, I looked like a balloon."

A spoiled, fat little boy, Ernie first experienced a change in the family fortunes at ten when his father, taking advantage of his connections on the force as well as Trenton's appetite for soft drinks, became a "beverage dealer" during prohibition. The family moved into the Parkside section of town to a 20-room mansion complete with stables, kennels, and a four-car garage. Ernie even had his own pony.

Because of good fortune, Ernie was placed in Miss Bowen's Private School, where his naturally inquisitive mind devoured knowledge rapidly. He took part in two plays in elementary school, and played the lead in "Old King Cole." His mother made a special trip to Philadelphia to a professional costumer, much to the chagrin of the teachers at the Parkside School who had to work hard to match her son's finery with their cheesecloth. Her interest in her son's career wasn't strictly limited to theater either; she also outfitted the whole eighth-grade baseball team with new uniforms.

All this came to a shattering end when Andrew's business bottomed out in 1935. Gone was the mansion and the pony. Ernie, who had already skipped two grades, entered Trenton High as a junior, and, though bright, was bored with public school academics. An indifferent student slated to graduate in 1936, he was held back another semester to make up failures in history, Latin, algebra, and chemistry. His abiding interest in the theater, coupled with a splendid baritone voice led to his joining the production of *HMS Pinafore,* where he had his fateful meeting with Van Kirk.

In the fall of 1937, Ernie returned to THS for post-graduate work and joined the chorus again, then doing *The Pirates of Penzance.* He briefly made friends with the accompanist, Eddie Hatrak, also a post-graduate student with whom he would work, a few years later, on Trenton's local radio station WTTM. Hatrak eventually went to Juilliard but returned to Trenton in 1941.

Since Ernie had distinguished himself admirably in *HMS Pinafore,* Van felt he would do well in the role of the Pirate King in *Penzance.* The matter was broached with characteristic delicacy:

"Do you sing?"

"No, not really," replied Ernie.

"Never say that," replied Van. "As of now, you sing."

Ernie would use that rationale many times in his future work.

The *Pirates of Penzance* proved to be a great triumph for Ernie. Van, encouraged by Ernie's natural ability, managed to secure a full scholarship for his prize pupil at the John Drew Memorial Theater in Easthampton, Long Island where he was directing. It was a summer filled with walk-ons, supporting roles, and second leads. Ernie appeared in *Green Grow the Lilacs, Stage Door, The Frogs,* and was second lead in *Arms and the Man* for which he received his first bad notice. A critic called him a ham. "All that remark shows is that critics aren't as smart as they should be," noted Van. "Ernie never overacted. His personality was such that he simply overpowered everybody, even in a small part. He couldn't have played it down; it wouldn't have been Ernie."

During that summer, Ernie also learned other aspects of the actor's trade. He enthusiastically participated in the interminable, post-curtain poker games, and watched city-slicker actors, who kept notebooks of their winnings, clean him out night after night. Ernie had been playing poker since he was 11, but more than once during his stint in summer stock he had lost his week's salary.

Again through the good offices of Van, he received a scholarship from the American Academy of Dramatic Arts in New York. His circumstances in Trenton had been mean but liveable. New York, however, became an unspeakable ordeal. He moved into a $4-a-week room in a fifth-floor walkup on West 74th Street, and was still naïve enough to be shocked when his landlady and some of her daughters were busted for running a whorehouse directly below his room. He was so poor that he could barely afford a loaf of bread a day. When he wanted a hot meal he heated up water, dropped the bread in and made gruel. He learned firsthand about Nedicks with its real citrus-ade atmosphere, combination cream-cheese-and-peanut-butter sandwich for a nickel, and the seven-cent coffee.

When he tired of gruel and the Orange Room, Ernie would starve himself for a few days to save up 35 cents for a night out: a 20-cent plate of spaghetti (with a nickel tip), and a movie. He had to move quickly by crosstown bus, for the poverty flickers (his chosen theater) charged ten cents before 7 o'clock. At those prices he never expected much. "Usually it was the life of Beethoven," recalled Ernie later on. "I saw that seven times."

Memories of those scuffling days survived in Ernie's cheapo spectaculars for radio and television:

Yes, Passionata *is the moving story of a pianist and his father who was a piano mover.* Passionata *will make you gasp with fear . . . you'll gasp when little Amadeus Trebleclef fights the two insane Chinese laundry men when they feed poisoned lichee nuts to his pet mongoose.*

It wasn't the grinding poverty that nagged him as much as not really knowing what to do with himself. Once you'd been to all the free entertainment, what was left? He returned briefly to Trenton for some Depression theatrics before another summer in Easthampton in 1938. During his second year at the American Academy, his health began to fail, and the following summer while working in Vermont, he collapsed, stricken with pleurisy complicated by pneumonia. All those late-night poker games, the nutritionless spaghetti dinners, and the five-flight walk-up had taken their toll. Even if Ernie had wanted to return home, there was no home to speak of since his parents were separated. Thus he found himself on Welfare Island where he began what he later called "The Welfare Island Engagement," in the terminal ward close to death.

Ernie wound up performing daily and nightly for enthusiastic audiences of doctors and patients. He was once wheeled into the fluoroscope room for a routine examination of his lungs. When the attendant switched on the lamps, he found stenciled on Ernie's chest in aluminum the words "Out to Lunch." Although he always looked like he was a candidate for Potter's Field, he managed to keep the staff amused. He organized checker tournaments for left-handed players with three or more gallstones and poker games for anemics whose pulse could break a hundred.

The ward in which Ernie first resided contained about a hundred beds, and, being a newcomer, he was placed near the door. As he inexorably moved toward the window through the attrition of his peers, he gradually became aware of the sound of carpenters working outside the window. When he finally reached a window bed and looked out, he learned that indeed carpenters were at work, not building houses, but coffins! There were dozens piled against the wall. Ernie put his face against the glass and hollered as loud as he dared, "Which one has my name on it!!"

"All the time I was supposed to be dying. The only thing the docs couldn't figure out was why I didn't hurry up about it." He would have probably been thrown out of Welfare Island for malingering if it had not been for the timely intervention of Van, who, having returned to the United States in 1940 after a sabbatical in England, arranged for Ernie's transfer to a sanatorium in Browns Mills, New Jersey. Through a subscription raised by other friends, Ernie received a radio to wile away the hours and a small allowance as well. The money no doubt went to poker, while the radio stayed tuned to WQXR, a New York City classical-music station. Between the cadenzas, Ernie entered and won many radio contests.

Though Browns Mills was closer to home and a less depressing environment, Ernie still rebelled against hospital restrictions. He was forbidden to smoke cigars that would damage his tender lungs. The doctors were less than sympathetic to the fact that he was utterly devoted to the habit since age 16. Andrew, good father that he was, smuggled the precious tubes of tobacco to his son anyway. Ernie had been hospitalized for nearly 18 months by early 1941, when the hunting season approached.

If the doctors were concerned about his smoking, one can imagine how they reacted to his walking. But Ernie didn't ask them. Andrew came to the rescue again and smuggled in a shotgun suitable for small game. At the earliest possible moment, Ern, pajamas under raincoat, slipped out and into the woods for a solitary day of shooting in the southern Jersey scrub. The staff never knew. A few weeks later one of the doctors told him that since his recovery was progressing so splendidly he might be able to join the other clinging vines on the front lawn for some sun.

"Gee, that's great," said Ernie innocently enough.

Neither Dame Nicotine nor The Call of the Wild finally persuaded Kovacs to terminate his engagement at Browns Mills. Early in the summer of 1941, he took "French leave" of the sanatorium, opting for the footlights. Perhaps he would make some money, though, more importantly, he wanted to live again on the stage.

It was a shyster from Philly with a big car and a flashy blonde who enticed Kovacs from his sick bed with a $100 retainer. Such a simple deal — he wouldn't kid Ernie. Ernie would be the chief actor/director/producer for the Contemporary Players, a pickup dramatics group composed of Trenton High alumni. Ernie and the producer would split a percentage while the crew took the spare change. Why not?

They booked themselves into the Contemporary Club in downtown Trenton, an edifice long since destroyed by flames (the arsonists could easily have been the irate cast of *Dark Victory*, their first production). The kids sold tickets like bucket-shop professionals. On opening night the producer from Philadelphia ran off with the receipts, leaving Kovacs and crew holding the bag. Rumor had it that Ernie himself was in on the job and split the boodle. No way. For the duration of the summer season the Contemporary Players became the *Compulsory* Players. They owed everybody: Samuel French, the gas company, the costumer, the printer. Ernie was back in Trenton all right — back in hock.

But it was theater, no matter how straw hat, and it was experience! Ernie was indeed the whole show with moderate assistance. He played all the leads, directed, assembled the incidental music from his record collection, changed the lights when necessary and scouted properties. He improvised with public-domain works, turning them into plays, yet in characteristic fashion he never managed to write out the third acts, so each time they were performed they were different. According to his associates at the time, his tastes in props veered toward schlock realism. In his production of Thornton Wilder's *Our Town*, he substituted a real coffin for the imaginary one that Wilder had in mind for the graveyard scene, no doubt drawing on his fresh experiences at Welfare Island.

The Contemporary Players worked throughout the greater Trenton area with gusto. No house was too modest, no audience too small. They played *Dr. Jekyll and Mr. Hyde* in Bordontown, and with the first line Ernie heard echoes in the high school auditorium. He looked out and counted exactly four people. When he asked them whether they wanted refunds, the four were adamant. They'd come to see the production and demanded continuance.

By season's close, dreams of glitter gelt and Broadway openings faded. The grandiose proceeds, less assumed debts, was one string of Christmas lights that Ernie had donated to the company previously as a gift. Reality intruded itself and Ernie returned to his mother's apartment over a candystore, two rooms divided by a curtain where Mary plied her trade as a seamstress. As poor as she was, she always managed to feed her son properly — steak and Charlotte Russe. Afterward, Ernie always maintained that he'd rather eat steak and Charlotte Russe one night and starve the other six than eat hamburger seven nights. It figured.

Next he took a job in a drugstore in Princeton, New Jersey, to help out at home. Besides commuting an hour by car Kovacs-style (barrel-assing over county roads at breakneck speed), the job required a certain amount of physical exertion. His former doctors would have been horrified. Ernie worked in a *long* store, so long according to him that, "You got an hour for lunch, and they timed it from the minute you left the counter, not the time you walked out the front door." Surely, Hungarian hyperbole. The customers weren't to his liking either, forever changing their minds in mid-purchase at mid-store. "You'd think they'd walk to the back with you. Not a chance. You'd go get a thirty-nine-cent toothpaste and then they'd decide to buy the fifty-nine-cent tube.

Fortunately for everyone, including Ernie, the road work was short-lived. A clerk's position opened up closer to home in the central Trenton business district at the Rexall drugstore on the corner of State and Broad. It was a shorter store and almost as good as working in front of the footlights, for Ernie turned it into one continuous stand-up comedy act by dispensing quips to the customers, French perfume to his numerous girlfriends, and "squats" (contraband cigarettes) to his friend Van Kirk. He shocked and delighted the patrons with his freewheeling style, and raised more than a few eyebrows when he grew a Groucho mustache which only Bolsheviks and Germans wore, as everyone in wartime Trenton knew.

By that time, he attracted more friends sympathetic to his theatrical aspirations — like Sam Jacobs, ["The Old *Cetriolo*" (pronounced *jah-drool*),] a Trenton legend in his own right who was in the publishing business and had modest theatrical connections. Sam had known Ernie since Ernie was 14 and had witnessed the fall of the Contemporary Players. He encouraged his young friend, and took him to the Bucks County Playhouse in New Hope, Pennsylvania, to meet stars like Wallace Beery. Sam told Theram Bamburger, "Mr. Bamburger, I want you to meet a future star . . . some day this guy is going to make it big in the theater." Apparently Mr. Bamburger was unimpressed with Sam's press agentry, and when it was time to leave, Ernie turned to the assembled luminaries, pointed a youthful finger their way and said, "You'll be sorry."

Sam had also introduced Ernie to cigars at 14 and taught him the master-schnorrer techniques that had permitted him to live moderately well and publish a few newspapers. A few years later Ernie would surpass even Sam in that department. Along with Van Kirk, Sam was instrumental in helping young Kovacs weather his postponed adulthood.

Through a judicious set of circumstances and not a little luck, Van managed to arrange an audition for Ernie for the staff announcer's job at WTTM, Trenton's local radio station. As it turned out, none other than "Fast" Eddie Hatrak, recently returned from Juilliard, was the station's musical director. After a hilarious audition in which Ernie butchered a few news bulletins, he was hired for 15 minutes a day which turned into 30, then an hour, 5, 12, and eventually much later, 24. He started his regular duties as the host of a late-night DJ show with a simple format: twenty records in two hours plus commercials, time checks, and news. By the time Ernie got the hang of things, all the commercials were pushed off until the last five minutes with the hundred or so other minutes devoted to cutting up and ad libs. He and Hatrak used to read the comics, Ernie mimicking all the voices and Eddie tinkling the ivories. For the Dick Tracy strips Eddie, of course, played "Eighty-eight Keys."

The sponsors didn't seem to mind what Ernie did with their commercials, even if he ran them all together. They knew the audience was listening. Though, at times, Ernie created his own sponsors:

Ladies and Gentlemen, Bash's Foundation, manufacturers of Bash's Imported Sheep Dip, since the beginning of time, are proud to bring to you, the radio audience, the product of prestige: namely Bash's Imported Sheep Dip. To the Suburbanite, the dweller in Trenton, the man on the farm, the woman on South State Street, Bash's Imported Sheep Dip has been for generations the important and vital rung in their individual and specific ladders of success. In keeping with their monumental efforts at maintaining good taste, the Bash Foundation will not interrupt this program with commercials.

During his reign at WTTM from 1941 to 1950, Ernie worked his way up from announcer to director of special events with his own truck and $40 a week — net. He was famous for his stunts with the remote truck. One year he decided to cover Groundhog Day for his listeners. He and his engineer called 20 or 30 agencies before they finally found someone in Pennsylvania who could even find a groundhog hole. They stood in the snow about a half-hour waiting for the woodchuck to appear, and then gave up in disgust. "Frankly," said Kovacs, "he was lucky because if he had appeared, we were both ready to slug him with the end of the mike."

In 1948, as director of special events, Ernie arranged to take flying lessons at the local air field, carrying a wire recorder to broadcast the results. The lessons went fairly well until he broadcast his first solo which turned into such a nightmare that he never bothered to return to the wild blue and always seemed to prefer trains after that.

Ernie loved the offbeat remote. To get a rabbit's-eye view of hunting season, he took to the fields in a reinforced trench, capturing the sound of whizzing bullets. To demonstrate how it feels to be run down by a train, Kovacs and crew journeyed to the local Trenton yards. He lay down on the tracks but at the crucial moment lost his nerve. The audience heard the crunch of the microphone and Ernie was billed for a replacement. Once, while covering a major fire and recording five minutes of flames, Ernie remarked to his audience that it was getting a little warm where he was standing. Astutely he turned around in time to discover that not only had the flames burned his microphone cord to a crisp, but they were now in the process of claiming his shoes. Thinking of nothing more original than "I'm on fire!" he hastily beat a smoky retreat.

He was best at the ad lib and frequently quipped too fast for his listeners or the censors (if they could keep up with him). Sam Jacobs once introduced Ernie to Caspar Balsom, a dwarf who played in *The Wizard of Oz.* Ernie's intro was, "This is the frigid midget with the rigid digit." Ernie had a natural gift for language and could cannibalize from any argot.

Ernie was forever talking about *brodskys* on the air. "Get yourself these heavy-duty brodskys for home use, guaranteed not to spill, rend, or break — or double your money back." Few of his listeners knew what a brodsky was, even if they tripped over one. A brodsky was Kovacsian for brassiere. In his skits he often used the name Cowznowski as a surname, be it Hyman Cowznowski or Bessie Lou Cowznowski. The name was a corruption of *Mad Magazine's* Melvin Cownowski, the What-me-worry? Kid (later dubbed Alfred E. Newman). Melvin was named after none other than the distinguished Bernie Cownowski, a Ewing Township local who back in Ernie's day did radio commercials in Polish and English and was known as the Polka King.

Most endearing of Ernie's Trenton shows was Koffee with Kovacs, an early morning wake-up program, which featured school closings and news, many remotes, and skits. Despite the morning show, he was known as one of Trenton's original night people because of the schedule he kept. He used to interview night workers at local factories or dairies — nothing was too bizarre — and eventually his listeners thrived on such exotica as moos.

Neither was studio personnel exempt from Ernie's stunts, especially Tom Durand, the chief engineer. It was normal for Kovacs to practice golf shots in the studio's corridors, sometimes during or after his show. On one particular occasion just to get Durand upset, Ernie painted a Ping-Pong ball to resemble a golf ball, and cut it in half. Taping it with adhesive to the main studio window, he added a few artistic flash marks with a grease pencil to simulate cracks. As Durand walked into the studio, Ernie quickly raised and swung his niblick. Durand suffered a minor coronary.

Fun and games aside, WTTM served a variety of uses for Ernie's show business aspirations. As an interviewer of *Talk of the Town,* a regular afternoon feature, he came into contact with many show personalities who played the Trenton Armory or the various medium-time downtown theaters that were staging areas for Broadway. Conveniently located between the town's two leading hotels, the Stacey-Trent and the Hotel Hildebrecht, Kovacs just had to wait and the stars would come in off the streets. One evening while Sam was up chewing the fat, Paul Whiteman staggered in after a show at the Armory, half drunk and gassy from overindulgence. To ease the agony of the ecstasy, so to speak, he used to take a high colonic enema. He yelled down, "Ernie, get the enema ready," but Kovacs and Jacobs substituted two bottles of Budweiser for the normal ingredients, and Whiteman had the thrill of his life.

The station's location was also convenient for Ernie's own night life, especially the Hildebrecht's jolly nitery. As a freelance member of the fourth estate, he spent more than a few nights with the boys being on top of everything. A man about town? Hardly. At 25 he was still an innocent, having been deprived of a normal or stable childhood. Moreover the illness had taken more years. The critical faculties that most men develop by 25 had eluded him. Nominally, he was still living at home with mother and desperately wanted to join the ranks of married men. Considering his emotional immaturity, it was not in his best interests to get married, though there was no one he respected who would tell him so and no one big enough. Impulsively he courted and married Bette Wilcox, a black-haired dancer he'd met at a USO show at the Hotel Hildebrecht. They were married August 13, 1945, and temporarily moved in with mother. Now there was one more mouth at home to feed.

Simultaneous with the happy event, Sam Jacobs offered Ernie a column on his newest venture, *The Trentonian,* a weak weekly with a shoestring budget. There was no pay for writing "Kovacs Unlimited," a series of plugs strung together with connectives, but there was always free food. Sam once sent Ernie out to interview the owner of a local diner, and Ernie brought along six hungry friends. The owner was flabbergasted. "Ernie, what are you trying to do, bring your whole meshpucha here?" Typical — and easy.

Sam and Ernie's master coup was free cigars, for they both had awesome habits; Ernie alone consumed between 10 to 15 a day. Sam worked out a deal with the Henry Clay Bark Division of American Tobacco — cigars for printer's ink. Each week they repaired to the plant just off South Broad Street near Chestnut in Trenton and looked up a certain Mr. Moscowitz. For one little plug in the paper, our boys received 100 cigars a week — gratis.

Sam's involvement with *The Trentonian* terminated in 1946 when it became a daily published by the Intertype Corporation then affiliated with the International Typographical Union. Kovacs, already a staunch union man, earned $50 extra a week doing the union's broadcast for WTTM. He joined the staff as a contributor with "Kovacs," a column that appeared on the funny pages adorned with Ernie's own drawing of a man milking Gertrude the cow from the wrong direction. Not that it made any difference to the readers or "ridders," as they were to be known. To his numerous hats of soda jerker, cigar salesman, radio announcer, and public servant was added "Ernie Kovacs — Kolimnst — er, Columnist."

An exponent of Hearstian yellow journalism, *The Trentonian* in its revivified state was a pastiche of sensationalist headlines, gruesome murders, gruesome photos of gruesome murders, housing scandals, tales of corrupt government, plus the comics and the ball scores. Kovacs wrote scrappy proz — prose — for the daily, and managed to catch the eyes of those without ears in the town. A sloppy, informal, somewhat libelous exercise in quippery, gossip, and plugola, "Kovacs" served a variety of functions for Ernie's numerous hustles. Since he earned 25 cents a column-inch, he manufactured controversy. He once attacked people signing the Pledge of Allegiance at an Armory show, and was deluged with letters, all of which he printed. Nothing was sacred:

Rudy Vallee anyone?
A very lousy skit on the Rudy Vallee show Tuesday night. Franlastically stinkoo . . . The Vallee show is a bit weak anyhoo and the audience is just about as sharp as a plate of half-jellied borscht.

Margaret Truman's singing debut:

Well, poor Margaret Truman has run the gamut and when the end of the literary gamut is run, the runner ends at this column. We like to think of oneself as the bottom rung of literature. (Some of our writer-inners have found a new rung below this one, but we won't have time to discuss it.) We feel that Miss Stickler (her teacher) and Karl Krueger (conductor of the Detroit Symphony) might have exercised better judgment in barring Miss Truman to a well-honed public. We cannot help but admire her courage in doing the broadcast.

Perry Como the krooner was regularly defended and attacked with italicized comments:

Oh yes, the singers and masters of ceremony from Trenton are rated very low by you (see how nice we are). I myself think they are very good, but why, Mr. Kovacs, do you continually criticize Perry Como (well one reason, he's miserable.)

which eventually drove one irate Como fan to surreptitiously deflate the front tires of the Kovacs limo one morning. A page-one insert photo in the paper, captioned "Rhapsody in Blew" (whew!) showed Ernie, pipe in mouth, salvaging some of his ride. Thereafter, he managed to steer clear of Como fans — almost:

Well, we finally found something nice to say about Como. Marion Hutton, who is replacing Perry on his much-needed (by us) vacation, is even worse.

Ernie attacked, lampooned, lanced, shredded, and punctured just about everything that normal Trentonians took for granted in their lives. Advertising with its hackneyed images of connubial bliss were frequent targets: an especially deadly campaign was the popular Campbell Soup image of the hungry husband with the clever wife.

Buster, that gal is not just clever, she is the local Rasputin. Open letter to F.W. [ed. note: Bette, the First Wife or Favorite Wife] Cookie, if we ever happen to throw open the door with a hungry shout on our moonlike kisses, and should a can of zup be open and ready, ditch it someplace and just say you didn't feel like cooking.

When he had enough time to think of something really witty, he invented print characters like Aunt Torchy, the crochety old lady who zinged 'em in on small-town hypocrisies.

Aunt Torchy says:

It's easy to spot a phony but they change the rules with each generation and you gotta keep up-to-date with the new rules ... This year's phony is the guy who tells everyone he's on the waiting list for Cadillac convertibles ... Knows danged well the waiting list is the safest place to be when you can't afford that sooper jaloppie.

Or smart aphorisms for the cosmopolitan observer:

Foo Philosophies No. 268½: a bird in the hand is worth two from the balcony.

and when on, he was brilliant and black-humored:

We take a peek into our portable plastic ball at the future. A radio station is going on the air ... The red light goes on ... The announcer says, "A very good morning, ladies and gentlemen . . . This is WA to Z the Alphabet Soup Network, going on the air. The first hour of broadcasting is sponsored by the Dunka Company ... Dunka, the only caffeine with coffee completely removed ... Remember, if you have doughnuts and coffee, don't hesitate to Dunka. The two hours following the Dunka program are sponsored by Ebony Soap Corporation ... Ebony, the all-black soap that conceals your blackheads. Remember to ask for Ebony ... It doesn't float, it doesn't do fine things . . . it's lousy soap, but it looks grand on your sink." Ebony, the maker of Zud, the soap powder that does everything ...

cleans teeth, spot welds, tightens leaky faucets, kills ants, roaches, and lice . . . The experimental laboratories of Zud are working on a new Zud feature, in fact, we may soon *be able to make the announcement that Zud washes clothes!*

And now Zud presents "Texas Dallas." This program seeks the answer to the question on every woman's lips "Can a Woman of thirty-three find teen-age romance?" The regular round table forum today will seek an answer to the question of the week "Do wife-beaters make good husbands?" . . . And so, Station WA to Z leaves the air for a complete day of silence . . . The remaining portion of our broadcast is sponsored by the Eureka Ear Trumpet Company . . . Remember their slogan "We can't all be Harry James but we can *own a Eureka Ear Trumpet."*

Between the radio station and the column, there was no element of Ernie's personal life that wasn't public business. If you lived in Trenton during the Forties, you lived with Ernie. Besides bits of humor, gossip, and plugs, Ernie also championed the condition of the city's restaurants, racial equality, pension parity, the plight of convicts — and even rented himself an apartment — or tried to.

We know you have troubles of your own, and we don't want to seem like we're protroodin' . . . But . . .
DO YOU HAVE AN APARTMENT, BUNGALOW, OR HOUSE FOR RENT FOR THE F.W., A FUTURE TINY-FEET-PATTER AND US (ME)?
We don't want to appear selfish in taking an inch or two of the column for ourselves, but having done it for some of our ridders, we're hoping you'll forgive us once and a while . . . if we can dig up the down payment we'll buy the place . . . signed one very despirate kolimnist.

The spelling in the kollim — kolum? — in the paper appeared a little unorthodox to some, but considering the

A musical "non-clue" from *Take A Good Look,* which even kept Edie in the dark.

ERNIE KOVACS DEPT. PART I

Strangely Believe It!

PICTURES BY WALLACE WOOD

CONTRARY TO POPULAR OPINION, **WAVING A RED FLAG** AT A **BULL** DOES **NOT** IRRITATE HIM!

ACTUALLY **COWS** ARE THE ONES WHO GET IRRITATED WHEN A RED FLAG IS WAVED AT THEM.

The reason a BULL gets mad when a RED FLAG is waved at him is because he dislikes being mistaken for a COW.

ARMAND K. FRECHETTE

A **FUR TRAPPER** from GRANDEBOUCHE, Canada,

TRAPPED A SINGLE MINK WORTH **$8000.00**

IT WAS DRAPED OVER THE BACK OF A CHAIR AT THE STORK CLUB.

Although a pound of **SALAMI** and a pound of **LIVERWURST** weigh **EXACTLY THE SAME,** THREE POUNDS of **CHOPPED LIVER** weighs more than both put together.

ARTHUR K. LIMBISH

a little known **COMEDY WRITER** MEMORIZED THE TAG LINES FOR OVER **930,000** JOKES

THE REASON ARTHUR IS A LITTLE KNOWN COMEDY WRITER IS HE NEVER LEARNED THE SET-UP LINES.

THE FANTASTIC ODDS OF **10,000 TO ONE** WERE LEVELED AGAINST **"FIREBRAND"** WINNING THE EPSOM DOWNS DERBY STEEPLECHASE IN 1938

"FIREBRAND" WAS A GARTER SNAKE.

ALTHOUGH THE **MOON** IS ONLY ONE **49TH** THE SIZE OF THE **EARTH,** IT IS **FURTHER AWAY!**

A MAN TRAVELLING ON FOOT FROM **TOKYO,** JAPAN, TO **SAN DIEGO,** CALIFORNIA

... WILL DROWN BEFORE HE GOES A HUNDRED MILES

***Pioneer* . . . early American who was lucky enough to find his way out of the woods.

ERNIE KOVACS DEPT. PART II

Strangely Believe It!

PICTURES BY WALLACE WOOD

AT EXACTLY **MIDNIGHT** IN **NEW YORK CITY** WHEN THE MOON IS FULL, AND THERE ARE NO CLOUDS IN THE SKY WHATSOEVER, IF A MAN WERE TO STAND ON THE **OBSERVATORY TOWER** OF THE **EMPIRE STATE BUILDING**

HE'D HAVE GOTTEN THERE BY ILLEGAL ENTRY AS THE TOWER CLOSES AT TEN P.M.

THE STRANGEST **SCIENTIFIC PHENOMENON** OF **ALL TIME** WAS RECORDED ON **MAY 18, 1956**, WHEN **ELIZABETH DONAHUE FORSNEY** WAS BORN IN A COMMERCIAL AIRLINER WHILE TRAVELLING OVER GRAND CANYON, COLORADO.

A TELEGRAM WAS IMMEDIATELY DISPATCHED TO ELIZABETH'S MOTHER WHO HAD MISSED THE PLANE IN DENVER.

On April 6, 1897, the 90-ton Barkentine **"MAJORCA"** DISAPPEARED DURING A NORTH ATLANTIC STORM... SEVEN YEARS LATER TO THE DAY, THE RESIDENTS OF THE SEAPORT TOWN OF BATON ROUGE, MASS, SAW A STRANGE SIGHT... THE MAYOR, CLAD IN HIS UNDERWEAR WAS CHASING THE WIFE OF THE LOCAL BUTCHER DOWN THE STREET WITH A CLEAVER.

A **FLOUNDER** DOES **NOT** SPAWN **CHILDREN**

IT SPAWNS BABY FLOUNDERS

MRS. ARNOLD FRUMKIN of Liver Bile, Ark. **RAISED** A **CAT**, A **RAT**, A **RATTLESNAKE**, AND A **RACCOON** AS **PETS**

Bless our home

IN AN APARTMENT ONLY **10 FEET SQUARE!**

... ODDLY ENOUGH, THE ANIMALS GOT ALONG VERY WELL, AND SHARED MRS. FRUMKIN EQUALLY...

GEORGE "CANVASBACK" JONES a Prizefighter from TOPEKA, KANSAS WAS **KNOCKED DOWN 34 TIMES** DURING **ONE FIGHT** ... AND THE FIGHT WAS **NOT STOPPED!**

George was fighting with his wife at the time.

***Cannibal* . . . person who likes to see other people stewed.

circumstances it was a miracle it went in at all. "Kovacs" came in haste to the typesetters, always on or near the midnight copy deadline. He was famous around *The Trentonian* city room for charging into its small two-by-four offices on Front Street, wearing pajamas under his trousers, ringing the bell out front for all it was worth, and screaming like Brett Baxter, star reporter, "stop the presses!" a sally to which the hardened compositors genially replied "gettouttahere, ya big moose." It must be said to their credit that they valiantly tried to correct Ernie's spelling when possible, but the "ridders" understood anyway — they had to.

There were other fringe benefits for *Trentonian* readers. When Ernie took vacations they could read guest dispatches by celebrities like Fibber McGee and Molly, Bob Hope, Jack Carson, Jack Benny, Bing Crosby, and — yes, even Perry Como.

Kovacs brought a certain cosmopolitan flavor to the state capital as well as a certain pride. He combined all those qualities in a stunt to end all stunts at the 1949 State Fair. Ernie didn't exactly plan to stay up for seven and a half days for the state fair, it happened spontaneously as a result of a quip to the program director when he saw his schedule for the week. "I might as well live at the fair grounds," said E. Knowing good publicity, Ernie's insomnia, and his crying need for money, the program director proposed that in exchange for the stunt, Ernie would receive an extra two weeks' paid vacation bonus. In addition to his regularly scheduled DJ show from 12 midnight to 9 A.M. and his popular "Talk of the Town" from 1:00 to 1:30 in the afternoon, Ernie was station-break announcer from 9:00 to 1:00 and stand-by announcer from 1:30 to midnight, periodically checking in to assure his audience that he was still awake.

The column was cranked out daily. Perforce though as the lance was tilted toward Morpheus to smash Milton

Berle's state record of 18 hours, the columns became more interspersed with ellipses and half-completed sentences. After seven full days of sleeplessness, living in a glass box on the fair grounds, Ernie's fortitude gave out and a few of his friends "assisted" him in the completion of the stunt. It is still discussed in Trenton.

By the late forties Kovacs was Trenton's most visible citizen. No event, charity function, or governor's ball was complete without Ernie, with or without his microphone. You couldn't miss him if you tried (he'd possibly miss you down on the streets). Some remember him stalking down the center-of-town streets wrapped in an opera cloak — Mephisto in spats. He was Trenton's Mister Cigar, a visible symbol of town solidarity, though personally he was less than solid for all his easy charm.

With his entrenched patters of consumption and his dark Hungarian temperament, getting married and moving back into his mother's house was a disastrous mistake. Being married was not the best solution for his problems. There were always fights between Bette and Mary over money — with Ernie in the middle. He was smart enough to keep working and out of the house. Financial problems compounded his already moody temperament, making him alternately sullen and explosive. He was always accusing his wife of cheating on him, but whether she did or did not was a moot point in the relationship.

Mary, who had exercised a more than unhealthy maternal concern for his welfare, was almost as bad as a wife. By 1947, Ernie and Bette moved from over the candystore into what he called in the paper "our ivy-covered rat hole" in Mercerville, New Jersey. He tried to play the part of the ardent husband in print, though a certain degree of bitchiness crept into his writing:

Some day when we collect some long, long overdue poker debts (Yoo-Hoo) we would like to invest in those fancy mo-om pitchers. We were torn between a television set and another electrical gadget for the F.W. last Christmas. But we decided on the other one and she tells us she'd much *rather have a washing machine anyway and she's glad we bought it. She was* so *happy in fact, she was crying. Even* cussin, *we recall.*

Start calling your wife Cookie in print and the saccharine sentimentality wears thin. Not that the marriage couldn't work; Bette and Ernie couldn't work within marriage. His only happiness was his two daughters. Bette Lee was born May 17, 1947, and Kippie was born January 5, 1949. Ernie was devoted to their welfare. Readers were apprised of the happy events in the column and treated to dissertations on fatherhood.

How to Change a Baby

First you must get your materials for one change: (1) a baby; (2) a belly band; (3) a nightgown; (4) a shirt; (5) a blanket; (6) several diapers; (7) one pair of bloodshot eyes, to be inserted in the place of those you normally use.

Ernie's extroverted media personality coupled with the "Our Town" atmosphere of the greater Trenton area made an increasingly impossible affair, and with the schedule he kept, what time did he have? When the children were old enough, Bette, a Daytona Beach native, took the girls down south for vacations, leaving Ernie, sometimes for as long as a month and a half.

With the F.W. and two progeny off to Florida for a month or so, we find ourselves the target for the Suspicious Eye. There is a friendly bevy of good folk très *anxious to report to the F.W. by Anonymous Mail when she returns. At the Lambertville Music Circus, a young lady selling gardenias approached us to change a five spot and we saw three notebooks appear in the hands of the standersby.*

The strains of the marriage continued to spill over into the pages of *The Trentonian*:

No New Jerseyite lives that agony we live with the Florida Chamber of Commerce. We firmly believe we have married the Chamber of Commerce. The F.W. comes from Daytona Beach and the most damnable situations have arisen in our three years of martial . . . er, marital bliss. We haven't tasted a Sunkist orange in three years . . . and the most agonizing experience above all is our futile attempt to convince the F.W. that Florida is having a hurricane when Florida is having a hurricane . . . She says she lived there "all her life" and never saw one . . . We've taken her to newsreels showing tropical palms being whipped around and she says it's nothin but lies. Honestly, we are not kidding . . . We actually have to go through this every time a storm hits Florida.

As the marriage deteriorated, Ernie made every attempt to salvage what little remained, if not for himself, at least for his offspring. He managed to buy a house, but in order to meet the $115 mortgage payments for his "rat hole" he took another job as the emcee for the Thursday night wrestling matches in the Trenton Armory. He thought that wrestling provided a little extra glamour, though he was beginning to tire of being Trenton's media cheese (or ham). He was working around the clock to support his lifestyle — compromising his tastes, the demands of the poker table, his wife and children's welfare. He was losing.

Despite the numerous demands made on his time, Kovacs still managed to act and teamed up with Bill Walker, a dramatics teacher at Junior High School 3 in Trenton, whose father had married Ernie and Bette in 1945. The Prospect Players were in need of a lead for Molière's *La Malade Imaginaire.* Walker chose Kovacs.

The Prospect Players were a step above the Contemporary Players of yore — no shyster producers with flashy blondes, no debts — just hard work. One week they would do *Hedda Gabbler,* the next *Ernest Slick From Pumpkin Crick,* or *La Malade Imaginaire,* or even the deathless *Ten Nights in a Barroom,* but not, thank heavens, *East Lynne.* That would have been curtains.

Bill and Ernie rotated the directorial duties and alternated leads, though Ernie was a case to direct. "You'd go out of your mind because he would get the whole theme of the show, the thread of the thing . . . but the tagline would never be there, so some of the people less adept at ad libbing than he was would be left onstage looking like fools while Ernie would pull out his cigar with his grin as though everybody else had forgotten his lines and, of course, nobody had — it was Ernie." Bill learned finally that either it was Ernie's show or no one's. A few years later when Ernie had his own troop, he would train them for the ad lib with directions like "When I flare my upstage nostril — watch out."

In 1949 his life was shattered when Bette deserted him, leaving Ernie alone with the children. For a while he was dashing back and forth, changing diapers, fixing meals, and generally going crazy hiring baby-sitters. He was determined to preserve their home at any cost. He made a temporary truce with his mother and she moved in to take care of the children. With his public life, Ernie was merely going through the motions. His friends tried to fix him up, but he was totally disinterested in women.

For the hell of it, he sent a wrestling tape to WPYZ, a small NBC-affiliated TV station in Philadelphia that was looking for a weekend announcer. They'd heard of his fame and accepted him without even listening to the tape. Ernie soon started commuting between Philadelphia and Trenton on weekends while the station figured out how best to use him. A few months afterward WPTZ made him host of *Deadline for Dinner,* an afternoon cooking show for lazy housewives. He was almost out of the nest now, but he had more catching up to do.

Code of E.E.F.M.S

1. An E.E.F.M. is a male.
   A — or a female
   B — or an interested in either political party.
2. An E.E.F.M. never sleeps later than 8:30.
   A — Unless he or she is deathly ill.
   B — Unless he or she is deathly . . . er, dead, that is.
3. An E.E.F.M. makes less than $987,648.23 per annum. (Slightly higher in the South and Southwest)
4. An E.E.F.M. may not raise ostriches or parsley for profit without permission of E.E.F.M.-1.

*Early Eyeball Fraternal Marching Society

e·e·f·m·s

EARLY EYEBALL FRATERNAL AND MARCHING SOCIETY

"3 TO GET READY"

EEFM

It's Been Real

EEFM-1

WPTZ CHANNEL 3

CODE OF THE

e·e·f·m·s

1. An EEFM is a male.
   A—Or a female.
   B—Or interested in either political party.
   C—Unless the EEFM is sleepy.

2. An EEFM never sleeps later than 8:03.
   A—Unless he or she is deathly ill.
   B—Unless he or she is deathly . . . er . . . dead, that is.

3. An EEFM makes less than $987,648,001.23 per annum. (Slightly higher in the South & Southwest.)

4. An EEFM may not raise ostriches or parsley for profit without written permission of Eefm-1.

Pass-word —"It's Been Real".

Kovacs premiered on Philadelphia TV on March 20, 1950, with *Deadline for Dinner,* soon nicknamed by Ernie "Dead Lion for Breakfast." The format was pure corn either way. The host held the spatula while some local culinary celebrity prepared his recipe. Ernie turned the show's format to his own devices, making the chefs the straightmen. One cook had the *chutzpah* to create a hamburger for Dead Lion which took a total of five minutes to shape, roll, and cook. What was Ernie going to do for the rest of the show? Ernie asked the smug gastronome what he would suggest serving along *with* the burger.

"Whatever you like," replied the chef.

"Well, for instance . . . ?" Kovacs insisted.

"Everybody likes something different," the man replied. "I wouldn't presume to tell people what to eat with their hamburgers."

"Listen," snarled Kovacs, "it doesn't take any mental giant to make a hamburger. Now what do you do to brighten them up?"

And on and on for 25 minutes, just in time for the next show. An ad lib by any other name would still smell like eggs Scavok. *Eggs Scavok?* Yes indeed, a famous Kovacs recipe concocted when no one showed up for the program (Scavok is Kovacs spelled backward). A masterpiece so vile it stank up the whole set after it boiled over during a commercial. Ernie called it an old family recipe and the technicians were forever wondering whose family it was. Eventually the station hired a permanent chef, Albert Mathis from Gulf Mills, an exclusive Mainline Philadelphia country club, to assist him. Mathis turned out to be such a perfect straightman that eventually they did commercials together.

Joe Behar, then 24, was Ernie's Philadelphia director for "Dead Lion" and all his other shows, though he did little more than shove Ernie in front of the camera, and hope for the best. What visual and culinary debauches transpired over the "Dead Lion's" two-year-plus run from March 20, 1950, to April, 1952, can best be left to the reader's imagination. Behar captures the show's spirit: "It was like what they do now when they do sketches about a cooking show and a guy gets loaded or makes a mess. That's what Ernie would do with him [Mathis]. He would try to make a dish and Ernie would just screw it up completely." Ernie would convey the directions almost right so that any housewife foolish enough to want to prepare a dish would have an approximate idea — approximate but never exact.

Stunned by the success of *Deadline,* the management placed Ernie on another show called *Pick Your Ideal,* which was enthusiastically described in one of the last *Trentonian* columns:

Yesterday (August 24, 1950) we started one of the most interestin' jobs we've ever tried . . . We have a new TV *show which began on Channel 3 . . . called* Pick Your Ideal *and there are* four *(4!) real, live, all female models on the show . . . Two lusch brunettes; Mary Lowell and Peggy Deegen; one scrumptsch blonde, Jean Wright, and "blond" Andy Anderson who does the fashion commentating. All we have to do is sit in the middle and smell four different brands of perfume as they collide somewhere in front of us.*

Hardly a memorable show and soon forgotten by everyone except the station management, who, instead of giving Ernie promotions to better shows, gave him more sleepers to resurrect. In November, 1950, he started *Three to Get Ready,* a wake-up show that started at — ugh! — 7:30 and haphazardly meandered to 9:00, Mondays through Fridays. With those hours, it didn't make sense to commute any more. Good-bye and a thousand thanks, Trenton, New Jersey.

To celebrate his auspicious entry into television for real, Ernie promptly moved himself into the recently vacated bachelor apartment of Joe Behar — and what a place! — right around the corner from the studio. TTGR had been using a wake-up format, providing weather information, news, and time checks for groggy Philadelphians. There was a clock in one portion of the screen and the news was dispensed via a cylinder with flipcards on the front of the desk. Ernie drew cartoons in time to the background music though he was never sure what kind of music it would be (at that ungodly hour neither was the musical director). Just for the hell of it one day, Ernie put a note on the cylinder offering two tickets to a rancid movie in Camden, absolutely the rankest giveaway in the station's history. To his surprise, the station was swamped with calls. Kovacs thought, "An audience? An audience!!," and the format became inevitably Kovacized. Between 35,000 and 60,000 people started tuning in for the morning's fun, and proved, in the words of one Philadelphia television critic, that "either some people are so anxious to watch TV that they'll get out of a sound sleep to turn on their receivers, or that the program is really worth watching."

Regular viewers learned to expect anything and everything on *Three to Get Ready* — Polish versions of *Mona Lisa,* Yiddish interpretations of *The Call of the Wild Goose.* The cartoons were sometimes discontiguous with the music, or perhaps the camera would focus on a wind-up toy. Then it happened! "I don't know exactly how it evolved," recalls Behar, "but one day, instead of throwing pictures on the cylinder, he started fooling around, so we kept the camera on him instead and he did some crazy things." Crazy things like conducting *The 1812 Overture* with progressively larger batons: a chair, a stuffed dummy; and when the cannons went off, a pillar. all ad lib.

After a while the records were replaced by the Tony de Simone Trio. Tony, the station's pianist/organist was assisted by his two brothers. Ernie easily integrated them into the show's new format. He dressed them in improvised costumes, danced with them, used them to open the show. It was Tony who developed Ernie's famous theme song originally called *Oriental Blues* by Jack Newton. Tony jacked up the tempo, added bells, sirens, and a rinky-tink piano, and created *Ernie's Tune* which opened and closed all his shows from then on.

Absolutely nothing was wasted on TTGR. There was no money to waste because there was no budget. Sound effects came courtesy of Bill Hoffman, the studio's sound librarian, who cued Ernie for many improvised numbers. Props were provided by Andy McKay, the production assistant and Ernie's partner in crime. Whenever there was an empty space, Andy would wing something to him from a huge pile of junk kept close to the set: a baby carriage, a rag doll, funny glasses, or a stuffed fish that Ernie once "caught" with the aid of the microphone boom. Once Andy threw out a pair of funny glasses with bulbous nose and buggy eyes attached. Ernie picked up a book of poetry and started reading with a lisp. One can safely conclude that Ernie's famous fag poet, Percy Dovetonsils, was born in the heat of the moment, or the heat of the heap on TTGR.

The most famous piece of junk was "Gertrude" or "Dirty Gertie," a six-foot rag doll that a viewer in New Jersey contributed from her attic. Gertrude was seen in various guises and various states of distress, thrown off catwalks, danced with, or stepped on. She literally got the stuffin's knocked out of her as an unpaid extra after a few months of abuse. Ernie sent out a distress call on the show and Gertie's donor came to the studios one morning to fix her on the air.

There was very little on *Three to Get Ready* that was normal, even though the format was ostensibly straight and supposed to provide valid information — news and weather. Poor Norman Brooks, the newsman. Only a flat separated Norman from Kovacs though it should have been a five-foot cement wall. Ernie used to climb up on a ladder and drip water on Norman's copy or on his head. The viewers could see the copy involuntarily jerk each time a drop splashed. Just for kicks, Ernie would adjust the studio clock a couple of minutes slow or fast. The poor newsman would unwittingly stretch five minutes of news into eight minutes or squeeze it into three. Ernie also attempted to depants him while on camera. And though he begged and pleaded with the management to either give him a separate studio or transfer him to less hazardous duty, nothing ever came of it.

TTGR had no pretensions whatsoever. Things were so casual that it was not uncommon for the camera to catch Ernie hurrying down Sansom Street to the studio. Since Behar already knew Ernie's route to work, he instructed the crew to aim the camera with zoom lens out the third-floor window. "He never realized it the first time," said Joe. "Then we shouted to him from the third floor, and when he saw it, he couldn't believe it. When he came into the studio, we picked him up in the elevator." Not only would the camera catch Ernie in the act of being late, it also followed him to the water cooler, into the master control room, and even outside, playing in the traffic.

When Ernie became used to the idea of continually being "on camera," he transformed his route into another set. One morning as he drove into sight, viewers were startled to see him towing a huge replica of Nipper, the RCA dog. They were even more startled when he stopped in front of a neighborhood barber shop for a shave and parked the pup by a fire hydrant. Without the benefit of sound, Ernie and his players staged many skits on Sansom Street despite some of the hidden dangers involved. Once Ernie as Herman Guggenflekker, senatorial candidate, came down the street in a horse-drawn wagon. Stopping to make a speech with the aid of cue cards, he promised his voters the works: a barrel of whiskey for each citizen; twelve pounds of putty, a plastic A-bomb. One of his constituents jovially heaved a pie at him. Unfortunately, it still contained the heavy metal plate. Mister Guggenflekker was knocked silly and suffered a contusion from that senatorial delusion.

The excavation for a future parking lot adjacent to the studio on 1619 Walnut Street was put to use by Ernie in a nearly fatal skit. Portraying a Chinaman who'd just tunneled through Peking and wound up in downtown Philadelphia, he slipped while getting out of the hole, plunged into a 14-foot cavity, and landed flat on his back in almost a foot of mud.

Staid Philadelphians were bent out of shape by Ernie's sight gags. They thought nothing of seeing bananas with zippered skins or apples containing plastic worms. They didn't blink when Ernie would pull a glass of water out of a tree trunk or a doorway. They thrilled to his daring impersonations of Doug Fairbanks, Jr. They ho-hummed when Ernie imitated warped records, or pretended, while inside a television set frame, that he was a picture that needed adjusting. And when things were slow, they could always do a close-up of his perfectly flexed left nostril.

Cheapo props necessitated cheapo camera tricks. By utilizing deceptive staging, there was no end to the possible visual combinations, like shooting an arrow into the air, "following" it quickly with fast panning until it rested neatly in an apple on Ernie's head: William Tell could do no better. By suggesting an off-camera monkey, Ernie could be an organ grinder, and after the camera followed the rope to its logical end, Ernie would be in monkey suit dancing with the ring attached. Once after Kovacs climbed a folding ladder, a stagehand nonchalantly appeared and removed the ladder, which left Ernie without any visible means of support except for the unseen rope to which he clung.

He once staged an interview with two men in a horse costume, where at its conclusion the camera discovered Kovacs in the back end of the costume. Ernie had merely switched places with the second man while the cameras were focused on the front of the horse.

Some sight gags really confused the home audience. With a pane of glass between himself and the camera, Kovacs proceeded to paint out the entire picture until there was only black. He also used the glass to lob eggs and custard pies at the audience just to make sure they were paying attention.

Ernie's own energy for ad lib naturally sparked his crews, ant TTGR produced some unheard of innovations using a variety of home-grown techniques. The standard camera at that time was the RCA Orthicon which was carefully designed to transmit a clear picture of whatever was in front of the lens. By placing a lighted can of Sterno just under the lens, a blurred effect similar to the fade-outs in movies was possible. Pieces of cardboard placed on the lens achieved a split-screen effect, and when a second camera superimposed another image in the blank space, further innovations were possible. If the background was neutral, Ernie could appear to be inside a milk bottle, provided one camera shot the milk bottle and another Ernie. His favorite trick was to "super" himself with a toy ship in the bottle and appear to be trapped while water was being added. After unsheathing an umbrella, he would take out a hammer and smash himself to freedom. The little-used horizontal reversal button on the Orthicon, which reversed the scan of the picture tube, made it possible for mirror images to be produced so that Ernie could stage interviews or even sword fights with himself.

Carl Weger, one of the engineers, developed a homemade inverter lens through the ingenious use of a soup can and two mirrors. It refracted and reflected any image to produce upside-down visuals. It was then possible for the cast to appear to walk across the ceiling, or have Ernie stage balancing acts with Gertrude, or even have the levitated magician's subjects (with the aid of black velour rope) do flips. Andy McKay conceived a skit where Ernie appeared to be vacuuming the ceiling of the studio.

The show's technicians had a ball with the reversed-polarity switch that worked like a photo negative, especially helpful when Ernie wanted to feign sickness with a bad cigar. Film editing, for more inventive skits, made Ernie's most famous Philadelphia stunt possible in which he played in a baseball game. No ordinary game either; for beside playing all the positions on both teams, Ernie appeared to be most of the spectators as well as the umpire and the hot-dog vendor. The film editing was augmented by "step printing" the use of every other frame of film plus the use of doubles. In 1951 this technical achievement was staggering.

And what of the sponsors? At first they were loathe to advertise. According to Roland V. Tooke, then WPTZ's program manager, "The advertisers wouldn't believe that people in anything other than the lunatic fringe wanted to watch TV from 7:30 to 9:00." Boy, were they wrong! The viewers, it appears, came in droves. One giveaway received 3,500 responses. A free shamrock offer induced 1,700 others to call in. At the time *Variety* noted that the show's ratings were 4.8 and as high as 7.2, which they deemed ". . . a remarkable dial-in for that early hour." Soon the advertisers came in droves too. The first week there were no sponsors, the second week 2. By the tenth week the number had risen to 24, and by the sixteenth week the number had grown to 57. In the last stages of its run, when the show was on for 7 1/2 weeks, there was an average of 50.

Even with this commercial success, Kovacs maintained his attitude in dealing with the sponsors. On the early WTTM shows he ran all the commercials together at the end of the show. No one was immune. A maker of barbecued chicken was shocked one morning to see his product ripped apart on the air, juices flying. A bakery that prided itself on the wholesome freshness of its doughnuts made the mistake of delivering some stale ones. Ernie took one bite and *boing!* he extracted a set of false teeth with the doughnut attached. Trigger Lund, a stalwart regular, snatched it away in a futile attempt to salvage the commercial, but met with a similar taste sensation. Meanwhile, Ernie's voice rambled on about ". . . the look of pleasure as this young man samples the very acme of the confectioner's art." Thereafter, the company in question sent a special man over with fresh hot doughnuts. They learned the hard way.

Meanwhile the critics were a little confused by what they saw at that mind-boggling hour. Merrill Panitt of the Philadelphia *Inquirer* managed to get up early one morning and concluded that TTGR ". . . was only less inhibited than a bunch of three-year-olds let loose in a candy store." Although he conceded that, "It's kind of a strange show, I'd like to review it some time but who can tell whether it's good or bad so early in the morning?" When Ernie read that he made up a banner which he stretched over the set: "Read Merrill Pannit in the Inquirer." So much for the fourth estate.

By May, 1951, the networks in New York were responding to Kovacs and TTGR's candy-store rompings. NBC and CBS enjoyed the people tramping across the ceiling and inquired specifically about the soup-can inverter. For a test, NBC assigned Ernie to his first network program, *It's Time for Ernie,* May 14 through June 29, 1951, at the innocuous time slot of 3:15 to 3:30. It wasn't much of a show since Kovacs was used to much more space: he barely had time to flare his nostrils. But to add insult to injury, WPTZ gave Ernie another cooking program, *Now You're Cooking,* which appeared locally once a week from May 15 through June 12. More work, more hours. Consider for a moment that *Dead Lion* still appeared twice a week from 2:00 to 2:30 and *It's Time for Ernie* was on five days a week — one hell of a schedule.

"We had as many as four shows running in a single day," said Andy McKay, "which kept us hopping from early morning to late in the evening with precious little time for private living. Luckily two of the shows were of the ad-lib variety, which didn't require much previous preparation. If there was any rehearsal, it was minimum — usually for the songs or the instrumental pieces. Skits were winged — we talked through the bits beforehand — and if cue cards were used, they usually stated the sequence of the business (exits, entrances, props, cues, etc.). With so many shows going on, spontaneity had to be the keynote."

Now You're Cooking folded in June but in August, NBC offered Ernie another show as the summer replacement for *Kukla, Fran and Ollie,* a popular children's show that appeared from 7:00 to 7:30 weekday evenings. *Ernie in Kovacsland* it was called. To celebrate his new status, he hired more personnel: one secretary, Angel McGrath, because he liked her legs, and one chanteuse, Eddythe Adams, also because he liked her legs and she was cheap talent.

Actually Ernie wasn't the first to notice Eddythe Adams. Joe Behar had seen her as an unsuccessful contestant on the *Arthur Godfrey Talent Scouts.*

At the time, Edie was a shy, retiring, nearsighted, sensational-looking blonde from a good family in Tenafly, New Jersey, who had studied opera at Juilliard. But, when she saw what "divas" looked like and discovered how much they earned, she opted for a theatrical career. Before her appearance with Godfrey, she'd won the title of Miss U.S. Television which entitled her to a walk-on on *The Milton Berle Show.* To further her chances for the big time and prep for the Godfrey show, she hired a knowledgeable Broadway coach who lowered her voice a few octaves and told her the secret of success: "Honey, it doesn't matter if you sing off-key or on-key — just move your mouth all over your face and look sexy." She learned Patti Page's inimitable "Would I Love You, Love You, Love You," and looked sexy, but lost anyway.

Originally Ernie wanted a Boo-boo-badoop chickie and thought Edie was too small, though after her audition he hired her.

When asked about her repertoire, Edie responded that she'd sing anything he'd like, but unfortunately her repertoire was actually limited to a few Patti Page songs. She was so nearsighted that she couldn't read cue cards and was forced to memorize all of her songs before the cast and crew showed up in the morning. "My job was supposed to be singer but what I really did was give Ernie a chance to think of what to do next," she said. When she was finished with a song, she'd throw Ernie a prop and be off. If her parents had any illusions about her big break in show business, they were mistaken. They were horrified the first time they saw her on the show, teeth blackened, taking a header with a custard pie.

Ernie taught her many tricks as a performer and comedienne. "I knew basic things, such as you're a spy and you're mad at 'X' because . . . and when I walk through a door, this is going to happen. There was never any script per se. You talked until Ernie was ready, and then he'd go for the laugh. We had certain signals. If he moved the upstage nostril, that meant 'stand still, I'm going for a joke.' Being nearsighted, I had to be close to him to see whether the nostril was going or not. So we had bigger signals when I was across the room when he was going for the laugh."

As for the secretary, Angel McGrath, her duties as Ernie's Gal Friday were far from typical and many times infuriatingly loose. She was responsible for typing and mimeographing what was loosely called the script, though actually it was no more than a page summary of what *might* happen, like "Ko blahs, blahs, blahs two minutes on loose livers, etc." She was also supposed to take notes on what transpired each day because many times the shows and the scripts were distant cousins. The notes were filed away for handy reference just in case anybody needed evidence.

Who needed evidence? Ernie needed the evidence. Even when using a relay of mechanical roosters beginning at 5 A.M. with an alarm clock, progressing to a buzzer, and finally a blaring radio, he sometimes failed to be roused. He'd leave the station at four in the morning and come back at seven. "I was a dead duck and I had a migraine for three years straight," he said years later. One morning his boss called him in for a chat:

"I saw your show this morning," said he, "you weren't funny."

"Do you know how many hours I'm on the air each week?" expostulated Ernie, "As much as some starts are in a whole season. I have no secretary [before Angel]. I run contests. I do my own writing. Do you honestly believe there's a human being alive, who's not encased in wax in the Smithsonian, who can be on thirteen hours a week and still be funny?"

The boss replied with equal aplomb, "I'm afraid you'll have to pick up your program, Kovacs, it sags."

Ernie was "sagging" moneywise. Added to his basic salary of $125, he was making an additional $25 apiece for the three other half-hour shows and a bonus of $5 per sponsor by the end of his *Dead Lion* daze. He wasn't going to be a millionaire by any stretch of the imagination at this rate. Besides, he'd told his readers in Trenton long ago that his taxman had scared him off:

Whatever happened to the American millionaire? Ain't no incentive to making a bundle these days . . . Always had a yen to be a millionaire, but Moe Balbresky, tax expert, tells us a man who makes six million would have less than a million after taxes. That's really tough . . . It's simply killed our ambition, that's all, killed our ambition.

He certainly wasn't going to make it through careful money management. He'd spend what he didn't have after he'd spent what he did have. "Whether he had it or he didn't have it, he always lived like he had it. He was always a very big liver whether he was making a thousand a week in Philadelphia or he was making one hundred thousand dollars out in Hollywood. It's unbelievable the way he spent money, it would just go through him like flour through a sieve," said Behar. In the early days, Ernie and the boys decided that they all should learn how to play golf, albeit none of them really *liked* the game. Ernie, of course, joined a country club while the others took to the driving range. A few weeks later Ernie invited them all to the club, and after suitably mangling the course during an afternoon of flog (golf spelled backward), they were treated to a stupendous banquet that Ernie provided, long before he was making the thousand a week.

And he still played cards. He never quit. "Oh god, did I play cards! Forever," said Joe. "He was such a compulsive player that he'd call to get a fourth at gin rummy at eleven o'clock at night and say, 'You gotta come down and play' and I'd say, 'Ernie, I'm sleeping,' and he'd say, 'Oh no, we gotta have a fourth, we got a terrific game going, we gotta have a fourth guy you know.'" Ernie was a persistent cuss and Joe would wearily get out of bed and take Ernie's money, for Ernie, though enthusiastic, was also the world's worst card player.

There used to be a weekly poker game back in those days at Ernie's apartment. Once somebody forgot to bring a card table and there were seven hands in the game, none of them knowing what to do.

"I know," said Ernie helpfully, "we'll play on the door."

"Which door?"

"The front door!"

Ernie unscrewed the front door, but there was no place to set it.

"Okay," said Ernie, "three of us will sit on the couch, and the other three guys will sit on chairs, and one guy on either end, and we'll sit the door on our laps."

"Like a goddamn sèance," said Behar, who then asked our hardened gambler what would happen if nature called.

"Well, we'll work it out, we'll work it out," replied Ernie.

Eight grown men sitting in a drafty apartment with a front door on their laps. "He just couldn't bear it. God forbid the game was going to get delayed for a half-hour," said Joe, reflecting back.

The networks had a much different relationship with Kovacs. They liked *Ernie in Kovacsland,* but they didn't like the idea that Ernie virtually ran the whole show. *They* were the professionals, and Kovacs needed *writers,* so they hired a few. They wrote, he rewrote. The first "Kovacsland" extravaganza followed the script all right — for about five minutes. The only things he couldn't screw up were filmed commercials. The staid New York *Times* remarked in a review of the show, "Kovacs seemed determined to knock the audience dead, even if he had to resort to using a pick axe." When one gets such reviews, they send you back to the bush leagues — Philadelphia in this case. The closing credits for *Ernie in Kovacsland* make that point abundantly clear:

THE ERNIE KOVACS SHOW NEVER DIES
IT JUST FADES OUT AND AWAY FROM
THE WPTZ STUDIOS OF PHILADELPHIA . . .

THE ERNIE KOVACS PHILE

THIS MESS WAS WRITTEN BY
Ernie Kovacs and Ollie Crawford.
THE MUSIC PLAYED BADLY BY
Tony di Simone and his Two School Companions
MISDIRECTED BY
Ben Squires
ALLEGEDLY PRODUCED BY
Ernie Kovacs
MISS ADAMS' CLOTHES BY
John Wanamaker, Philadelphia

Even with Ernie's considerable salary, Philadelphia was still the bush leagues, and just to teach him a lesson, WPTZ tacked another half-hour onto TTGR so the hours were 7:00 to 9:00 instead of 7:30 to 9:00. Now Ernie was really late in the mornings and Trig, Edie, and Andy were forced to schmooze on the air until Ernie staggered in. Edie would show up in curlers until the crew finally cured her of that habit by turning the camera on her.

During the final months of *Three to Get Ready,* the E.E.F.M.S.(the Early Eyeball Fraternal and Marching Society) was formed, brothers of the bleary eye, a sad-sack club of unfortunates who were working stiffs and Ernie's morning audience. The membership included people of all ages, especially school children. Just by asking, anybody was eligible to receive a handsome membership card with bloodshot eyeball emblazoned, signed by E E F M.-1, Ernie, or E.E.F.M.-2, Edie, depending on who answered the mail that morning. E.E.F.M.S. was a tradition, as was the phrase "It's been real," the E.E.F.M.S. password. According to McKay, "It was used as a sort of signature on all our shows. It cropped up everywhere and anywhere. It could appear on the side of a balloon, re-appear on a piano stool, on a wall, on someone's bald spot — that sort of thing. You never knew where to find it. All you had to tell the director was, 'It's over there.' Ernie never knew and Edie

Uncle Gruesome

Adams never knew." "It's been real" remained as much a characteristic of Kovacs as his ever-present cigar and mustache.

In November, 1951, Ernie was given another chance by the big boys with a show loosely patterned after Fred Allen's *Allen's Alley* and a time slot of 11:30 to noon. *Kovacs on the Korner* took place on the street and featured cute songs and patter by Pete the Cop, Alfred the Dog, Tondelayo (Marge Greene who was also one of the unfortunate writers), Little Johnny of Phillip Mor-ris-ssss fame, Ernie (who played himself) and Edie (who was allowed to sing once in a while). The show was more than unfortunate: it was dumb. With an introduction like the following, you can easily imagine what transpired:

Kovacs on the Korner . . . the place where the phrase "Give it back to the Indians" first began. — The members of our neighborhood tribe include that happy Irish warrior, Pete the Cop. That gal he's talking to isn't Pocahantas but Edie Adams, the thrush on the corner. Our three men in white, engaged to sweep the streets, work harder at trying to find ways to get out of work. They play musical instruments and call themselves the Dave Appel Trio. The guy dreaming is Cheddar, Ernie's chauffeur, who blazes more trails with Ernie's car than an Indian on the warpath. And there's Little Johnny, low man on the totem pole, and from the looks of things he's always ready to bury the hachet in somebody else's head! Over here is our — ugh! — Big Chief of the block . . . Ernie Kovacs . . . the white man's answer to Sitting Bull.

Needless to say, Ernie loathed this show and everything connected with it. Working on such an insane production merely exacerbated the public end of his life.

Television success in Philly brought him to the attention of many people, more than even he knew. Bette, his wife, returned from obscurity, after her desertion, to lay claim to him, his money, and the children. From November, 1951, to the summer of 1952, Ernie was embroiled in a divorce/custody battle so violent that it spilled over into the studios of WPTZ. Process servers ran through the sets like Keystone Kops looking for Ernie. One day, to avoid them, he decided not to show up for work. His persona was retained by a mysterious figure seated behind a screen, smoking a cigar. Eventually Ernie gained full custody of his children which guaranteed Bette visitation rights on Sundays and every other week in November, 1952. The court also stipulated that, " . . . said children be removed from the influence of Mrs. Mary Kovacs, parental grandmother."

One of the reasons that Ernie's marriage broke up, though certainly not the main one, was his mother. Ernie married to escape, but her proud dominance prevailed. She had helped him through many crises when Bette first left, though if we are to believe "The Old *Cetriolo*," Sam Jacobs, "Ernie's biggest aspiration was to leave Trenton because he couldn't stand his mother." Ernie used to complain to Sam about his wife and his mother on a regular basis. Mary was an extremely powerful influence in Ernie's early life — maybe too powerful. According to Sam, "Mother was domineering, tyrannical at times; she stunted his early development. Ernie at twenty-seven reached the success he should have achieved at fifteen." Although she was no longer Ernie's wife, Bette didn't want Mary to exercise the same influence over the children that she had exercised over their somewhat questionable connubial bliss. Mary remained offstage for the rest of Ernie's life.

On January 14, 1952, *Today* with Dave Garroway premiered on the NBC network from 7:00 to 9:00 weekday mornings, overlapping *Three to Get Ready*. Since *Today* was a special NBC project, the network was particularly anxious for all their affiliates to preempt their local shows, WPTZ included. After much hemming and hawing, *Three to Get Ready* breathed its last on March 28, 1952, with a tearful farewell, including guest appearances by Ernie's mother and his two children. But even before *Today*, Ernie was anxious to leave Philadelphia. The cooking shows were easily transferred to other hosts and *Kovacs on the Korner* was about to be given back to the network Indian givers. Dan Gallagher, a CBS producer, offered Ernie his own show in New York with a time slot of 12:45 to 1:30, and he bade adieu to his Philadelphia confrères and the NBC network geniuses.

In contradistinction to his performance on TTGR, Ernie paid *On the Korner* its just desserts. The last skit of the show called for a character (played by Marge Greene) to be put into a steamer trunk for a few minutes of hijinks, but Ernie, clever fellow that he was, instead of just shutting in Marge Greene, *nailed* her in, ignoring her screams. Afterward he proceeded to take a hammer and destroy the set, making sure that no one could resurrect it again.

He tried to take as many of his favorite cohorts as possible, but union regulations being so strict, only managed to take his actors, Trig, Edie, Andy, and Angel McGrath, the secretary. He plucked "Fast" Eddie Hatrak from WTTM and was off. The station's personnel were saddened by his departure. "Everything was just dull routine around here after he left," sad Bob Allis, one of the station technicians. "When Kovacs was around, everyone was creative. We were jealous of New York for having him."

Ernie's success on Philadelphia television was something very extraordinary. "We had latitude to use the TV medium then," said Andy McKay, "something which couldn't happen in today's formula-ridden world of TV. There was a fresh and, above all, adult approach which was inspiring and gave us all a sense of creativeness, of having furthered the medium along its true course, not aping radio or the stage." Roland Tooke, erstwhile program manager for WPTZ, stated the rest. "The industry no longer offers such an opportunity. It is now a world of time, budgets, ratings, sponsors, pressure groups, and play-it-safe programming. The result of the change is simple: an Ernie Kovacs coming along today wouldn't be allowed in front of a camera." *Kovachior, Kovachior,* New York beckoned a second time, and Kovacs would not be denied.

"One executive didn't go out to lunch so they spent some money on scenery."

— Note on *Kovacs Unlimited,* script — 6/22/52

"Where the hell did you get those?" exclaimed Eddie Hatrak after seeing Ernie's $250 special interview shoes purchased for CBS. Not that Ernie didn't trust Gallagher's word, he just wanted to make sure *they* knew this was no Philadelphia schnook they'd hired.

Gallagher delivered the job but precious little else. Ernie could as easily have been sleepwalking through another episode of *Three to Get Ready* with the stupendous budget he was afforded. Bright lights, indeed! If he was expecting the king's treatment for the lion's share of the work he'd done on WPTZ, he was mistaken. CBS assumed they'd hired the local eccentric (with or without the shoes) for the 12:45 to 1:30 weekly show, and Ernie wasn't about to disappoint them.

Kovacs Unlimited, emanating from CBS Studio 60, commenced April 21, 1952. Ernie had a deer's head hung over his desk, a few flats, some songs, an interview or two, and a skit. What can you do with 45 minutes when your only audience are shut-ins? For anybody else stranded in that time zone it would have been curtains, but Ernie was used to curtains — black velour curtains, if possible. Beside Gertude, who was still having the stuffings knocked out of her, the show starred that damned deer's head. Sometimes it would be smoking cigarettes, sometimes the cigarettes would be loaded — bang! And commercials? Try Lost Beer, or Briefie cigarettes, or Foop — the hair lotion that comes in a plier-shaped bottle.

Only the location changed. The scripts were as loose as before, though this time Trig, Andy, and Edie knew how to decipher Ernie's directions, even when they appeared like this:

KOVACS: *witty fellow that he is, regales the assembled crew with his factious — er, facetuous — er, fatuous — facititieous remorks on butchery. He will talk about slicing kidneys, beeves, and castrations in capitals aboard — er, abroad. (Actually, broads do not enter into this delicate surgury . . .)*
After this hilarious raconteur has killed everyone with laugh stuff, we bring in our Tenefly thrush, Miss Edyythe Adams, who will sing that old loveable tune . . .

Well, at least there was a song someplace . . . maybe. On the other hand, it was equally possible for Ernie to wing it entirely with directions like "somebody, think of something funny quickern' hell to fill in the last ten minutes — I quit."

The budget for this extravaganza, if used for personal expenses, would probably have taken care of only his daily cigar bill. "Eighty-eight Keys" Hatrak had more than a few scoring problems with an "orchestra" composed of a piano, a theremin, a cymbalum (Hungarian instrument like a zither), a violin, a male quartet, and two female vocalists. " . . . And we were supposed to do an orchestral number every week," said Hatrak, "so I would end up doing a series of solos." Ernie endeared himself to "Fast" Eddie once by asking for eight minutes of Martian music, whateverinhell that was, minutes before showtime.

As with *Three to Get Ready*, Ernie continued to innovate television humor. One of his early CBS routines was to take a popular song, show the lyrics, and accompany them with inappropriate visuals as with *The September Song*:

When I was a young man courting the gals I played me a waitgame	Drugstore-wolf whistling at passing girl. He is zoot-suit-type, 1890 era. They are both old-fashioned.
If a maid dissuaded me with tossing curls	Girl saying "no" throwing curls at man a few feet away (she is pulling curls off head and throwing them).
While I plied her with tears in the place of pearls	Necklace of tears on girl's neck she says, "Hey dese poils are wet!"

In the beginning there were few sponsors, so aside from his old faithfuls, Kovacs thought up some new products to interest his audience like Pancho Paganini's Pounds Off Pellets.

Are you on the plump side? Do bridge tables cringe when you deal? Madame, do you purchase your dresses in the stout males department? Do you use liner hausers for shoulder straps? Do your friends jam up in doorways with you? In short, do your associates call you "fatty"? Then it's time, it's high time you latched onto Pancho Paganini's Pounds Off Pellets for that excess avoirdupois. Here's a printed testimonial or two on the package from Chunky Hippads of Little Pebble, Arkansas: "Before I started taking Pancho Paganini's Pounds Off Pellets I used to weigh 487 pounds; after I took my first two-pound box of Paganini's Pellets, I weighed 489."

And more quiz shows. His most famous was a takeoff of *What's My Line*? called "Where Do Ya Worka, John?" Here the contestants never tried to fool the panel who were all sufficiently crazed types to begin with. The contestant, just to put the panel out of its misery, agreed to any occupation suggested. Kovacs played Mr. Brandy McGruk, bartender, dressed in bar apron, white shirt with black shirt garters, shot glass in pocket:

HATRAK: *Who is your favorite singer?*
ANDY: *What are your hobbies? Are you an amateur photographer? Do you prefer the old type of hobbies to modern ones?*
HATRAK: *What is your favorite method of transportation?*
EDIE: *Who is your favorite announcer?*
ANDY: *Do you play cards?*
HATRAK: *Do you see much comedy? Are you in favor of TV comedians?*
EDIE: *Where do you eat most of your meals in New York?*
ANDY: *When you die, have you thought about being cremated?*

HATRAK: *Are you perhaps an artist? Are you good with your hands?*
ANDY: *Are you connected with the theater? Did you have any partiality toward vaudeville or ballet?*
EDIE: *Oh, I know, you're from a baby-sitting service . .*
KOVACS: *Shucks, you're right* (he leaves).

New Yorkers soon enough became versed in Kovacsian linguistics just as their Philadelphia and Trenton counterparts had. His favorite word, *scavorkoroonie,* appeared in almost as many places as "It's been real," and it was almost as popular as his commercials for Lost Beer. The cheapo movie epics continued unabated as the names of the players stumbled toward new heights of absurdity like these for an anonymous spaghetti Western:

MILLING CITIZENS
Gregory Clinkhart
Milton Cavanaugh
Horace Greezy
Beechmont Goldfarb
Bessie Lederkrantz

NERO .... *Arlington Wesmack*
HIS BABE .... *Hecuba Baldspot*
MARCUS PARCUS .... *Heatcliff Coldsore*
PARCUS MARCUS ...... *Breathless Gregory La Planchee*

Eventually *Kovacs Unlimited* did find sponsors, but they fared no better in Ernie's hands. The makers of Flamingo Orange Juice had many occasions to rue the day that Ernie became their champion. On August 22, 1952, they were shattered with this one:
NOTE: This will take some doing and will necessitate fast changes . . . every blasted bit of prop and whatever will

Percy Dovetonsils

have to be exactly in place before we begin this . . . make positive sure that everything goes right this time . . .

1:15: *Trig and Andy stand in front of Greek set . . . snow is flying on them from behind set . . . flying, not dribbling . . . they are clutching at throats . . . Kovacs comes in on all fours . . . barking . . . he has Flamingo can around his neck . . . they look at him (he is wearing a dog collar) and then examine can . . . they hold can toward camera and we dolly in like a sonofabitch for c.u. . . . on tight c.u. we go into Flamingo film.*

Dunhill cigarettes, another victim, sometimes got an assist from Percy Dovetonsils, "Maybe some of my poems sound like a joke, but believe me it's heavenly when you inhale this smoke." In spite or because of himself, *Kovacs Unlimited* was sponsored by Oakite, Nylast, Swansdown Cakes, Dreem, Rybutol, BaBo Cleanser, and Alka-Seltzer, and they were nobody's fools, but his.

CBS technicians soon joined the fun. Russ Gaynor, the soundman, took over Bill Hoffman's function and improved the quality of the show significantly. When Ernie interviewed a blasting expert, he instructed Russ, "This guest will talk about blasting and riveting. I suggest you hold back on the blast for the right psychological moment and then scare the hell out of him with a super-doozie."

The soundman was an important part of the show; without him the sight gags went flat. Gaynor's timing made this commercial for El Softo Shampoo perfect. "Look at this lady who uses El Softo," said Ernie, running his large hands over Andy McKay's dope-wigged head to the accompaniment of a slow sandpaper scratch. He picks out a hair — *boing*! He bends it to show tensile strength; it sounds like a final snap of a rotten orange crate. When Kovacs casually threw it aside, Gaynor dropped an iron pipe. "Yes, El Softo. Look how well-groomed this young lady's hair has become with just one small application."

(c.u. of ingredient label: El Softo has no adulterants. El Softo is brewed from only the finest of raw materials. El Softo contains only medium-grade lard, pure creosote, crushed imported mothballs, homogenized catfish oil, diced yoghurt, and generous amounts of spiked kerosene.)

No wonder the hair clunked. The bottle for said commercial was actually a milkbottle filled with coke, lumps of putty, and pebbles, and capped with a rubberball stopper with the El Softo logo stenciled on top.

No show was immune, no convention above reproach. He parodied a nightclub interview show similar to *Playboy After Dark,* which emanated from the famous Stork Club. At the Crane Club, the genial host interviewed famous personalities who just happened to be on hand when the microphones were on and the camera running. Inevitably there was a mouthy sexpot who was just dying to be on camera while the host was trying to find someone he really wanted to talk to first. In fact, anyone else was preferable to being crushed by iron-plugs from the camera-struck wenchlet:

And now to your lovely movie star Lorelli Latour . . . by the way I see some famous people here at the Crane Club. There's Drusilla Litmus, editor of that famous gourmet magazine Acid Mouth. *And over there next to Herbert Moskovsky, I see Stacatto Trapezoid, the inventor of the nonelastic garter, whose book* Varicose Veins Can Be Fun *is a Book of the Year selection . . . and there is Mr. Skinhead Glarepate, affectionately known as Baldie, and nationally renown expert on growing hair. His book* Bangs Are a Fetish *is also a best seller.*

There was an abundance of puppet shows; Cromwell Cranston, semi-private eye and man-about-town, and the Kovacs gallery; some of the thousand faces of Percy Dovetonsils; Wolfgang von Sauerbraten, the German disk jockey; and all manner of interviews with the renowned J. Walter Puppybreath, a schlump who consistently endeavored to sell Tin Pan Alley solid gold tunes like *The Cockeyed Cockatoo from Canton Was a Gone Gone Goose on Roseshaun* to bored panelists.

Oh Little China boy went walking in the wood.
He was hunting for a bird to make a sandwich taste good.
He walkee all day, and walkee all noon.
He walkee all night by the light of the moon.
Then he saw a bird and what was he to do,
How was he to do it with a cock-eyed cockatoo.
He pickee up his rifle, and pullee trigger likee this:
(rifle shot)
Rifle goee off, but China boy he miss!
(man with pillow drops feathers on Ko)
Oh the cock-eyed cockatoo from old Canton was a gone gone goose on Roseshaun.
How was he to know, when he sat upon a twig that China boy stood by with bullets oh so big.
Oh, he tasted bird like that at New York's Ruby Foo.
He said this cockatoo, I will show a thing or two, so once again to shoulder risee up his little gun, he pullee trigger fast no feathers fall but one.
(rifle shot)
The cock-eyed cockatoo from Old Canton was a gone gone goose o Roseshaun.
Whether that cockatoo is not much meat, but plenty of fuzz and feather he no believe in legend so he pickee up his gun.
He pullee hard on trigger
(rifle shot)

and look into the tree, but the cock-eyed cockatoo sit there smiling down at he.
Oh, the cock-eyed cockatoo from old Canton was a gone gone goose from Roseshaun.
By now Chinese boy is hungry and pain is in his bones, so he fillee up his rifle with lots of little stones.
He aimee up his rifle and watch so carefully, to get a shot at cockatoo, smiling in the tree.
He say, I no hittee him, I surley

(rifle shot)

going to cry.
He then pullee trigger.
Oh the cock-eyed cockatoo from old Canton was a gone gone goose on Roseshaun.

(man drops entire bag of feathers on Ko)

"Well a good try, J. Walter Puppybreath, but I'm afraid the panel didn't pass on your song."

The mid-morning show was just too much for the network, let alone the audience. On December 29, 1952, they shunted him back into his familiar limbo in the centrally stranded time zone of 8:30 to 9:30, weekdays. Gallagher by this time had given way to a succession of producers like Ned Cramer, Frank Moriarity, and Chuck Hinds. Whether they were more successful at controlling Kovacs than Joe Behar had been in Philadelphia was debatable. All shows still bore the legend "Written and Directed by Ernie Kovacs."

CBS wasn't completely setting Kovacs aside. They decided to put him on Tuesday evenings from 8:00 to 9:00, to see if they could draw viewers away from the leading competition of the day, *The Milton Berle Show.* Commencing December 20, 1952, and billed as "the shortest hour in television," Ernie tried to break Berle's firm hold on the Trendix ratings, but had to give up April 4, 1953. Meanwhile the morning show was surviving. Edie Adams was appearing on Broadway in *Wonderful Town,* and a parade of female singers attempted to replace her with varying degrees of success.

Whatever visual tricks he'd developed in Phillie were perfected on CBS. The Kovacs-under-Glass number with supers and black velour background was augmented by goldfish swimming placidly as Ko fought for air space.

The repeated use of film clips and split-screen prestidigitation produced one masterpiece where Ernie pulled a lever marked "Do Not Touch," and was almost run down by a train (*stage left*). A few minutes later he came back to the lever "Do Not Touch . . . Honest," and again pulled the lever. Four trains converged. The third time he didn't even touch the lever, but calmly walked to his assigned spot to wait. Then the inevitable came, he stood sideways and pushed the trains back; he then walked back to his desk to continue the show.

Providence provided Frank Yasah, a gentleman with Coke bottles for glasses, to assist Ernie with special effects at CBS. Frank developed the lustra light, or black light, which Ernie used and re-used with vigor and imagination. After treating a surface with special chemicals sensitive to the black light, it was possible for pianist Hatrak's body to disappear, leaving his hands to play the cadenzas. Frank's device, combined with Ernie's ingenuity, produced a chess-game ballet where the dancers resembled chess pieces. The board and pieces were both treated so that sometimes the board would disappear, and the pieces would scramble around madly to find their proper positions. The board could even change colors.

Assisting Gaynor and Yasah were actors Trigger Lund and Andy McKay, who'd been Ernie's henchmen in Philadelphia. Both were indispensable members of the Kovacs team, though Andy had a special gift all his own. He was a master in the art of the spiral faint and an expert at comic crying. His flopping around would always be good for a few minutes of shooting time during the course of an ad-lib show. Kovacs once made a backhanded compliment to Andy when he was giving directions for a "normal" bogus commercial for a new soap. A housewife is bending over her washtub when her son (Andy) comes in laughing and cutting up. The old lady looks up disgustedly, whips out a revolver, and plugs the kid between the eyes as Ernie intones, "Are you out of sorts on wash day? Maybe it's the soap you're using . . ." Kovacs in the script cautioned Andy to play it straight, "He dies . . . one motion . . . no spiral faints . . . no clutching . . . no nothing . . . just die . . . as unspectacularly as possible, and he lies still without moving . . . does not put lily on chest . . . no request for cremation . . . just dies . . . Plain D.I.E., Die." Trig and Andy were also responsible for a weekly pseudo-documentary called the "Year War," like *You Are There,* which featured a few dance numbers interspersed with film clips from the studio's film library.

CBS "early eyeballs" also saw the premiere of a Dovetonsils classic. A simpering deadpan version of:

ODE TO THE MAN WHO FELL OFF THE EMPIRE STATE BUILDING

I see the guard has left me now — the tourists are looking West
I think those tours are somewhat dull — this solo stuff is best.
I'll climb upon this narrow ledge — 'tis not too wide, the poet quipt.
Perhaps I should get off before, oh darn, now I've gone and slipped.
Dear Me, off I go into outer space, 103 floors to fall to —
Let me see . . . am I correct or is it 102?
Never mind it's of small concern. I'm falling anyway
I hope I clear the eighty-sixth, it seems to be in the way.
There, I've missed the eighty-sixth, not all do that fall,
I think for my first go at this I've not done bad at all.

Say, that typist on the seventy-ninth is waving to me, that's a bit of luck.
Well I'm still falling, now let me see, I'm at the sixty-third.
It's started to rain, it's dampish out here, I'm glad I'm not a bird,
I wouldn't care to do this kind of thing too often over town.
I'm so uncomfie way out here, there's no place to sit down.
Oh there goes thirty-seven, I have my office there. I should have the lamps out; my light bill is a bear.
It's rather nice out though today, I'll take a peek. Sakes alive!
There's George Thompson, awfully nice chap, wonder what he's doing on twenty-five?
It's nicer down here than higher places.
At least I'm beginning to see some other faces.
Say, look at them run, oh see how they scatter.
Guess the rumor's around that I'm likely to splatter.

But wait — *Kovacs Unlimited* did provide news as per its format. "The Pathetic News," captured what most viewers would have preferred to forget that hour in the morning. Billed as the "Eyes, Ears, Throat and Nose of the World," the "Pathetic News" highlighted the surrealist news of the week:

CLYDE BAGLEY, NOTED LION TAMER, COMPLETES BOOK
LION TAMING CAN BE FUN

KOVACS: *In Miami, Illinois, last week Clyde Bagley, the famous lion tamer, had finished his book involving a new theory of lion taming. In his new book, Mr. Bagley advocates taming lions without the use of gun, chair, or whip. To quote Mr. Bagley, "Just show lion who's boss."*

After Mr. Bagley completed his book, he volunteered to illustrate his method of lion taming without use of gun, chair, or whip for our Pathetic News cameramen. At twelve noon Mr. Bagley stepped into the cage and at twelve fifteen the Pathetic cameras were turned on the scene.

(r.p. of interior of lion's cage, circus-like if possible. Lion is sitting on small stool back of small table. He has a knife and fork in his hand and a plate in front of him. Beside him on the floor are two black, shiny, lion tamer's boots lying on top of one another. Lion has napkin tied around his neck. As we take picture, lion puts up large book on cover of which in large lettered art work *Lion Taming Can Be Fun* and in smaller letters: CLYDE BAGLEY)

CBS was still unimpressed so *Kovacs Unlimited* and *The Ernie Kovacs Show* died — no spiral faints, no lilies on the chest. On April 14, 1953, the wake was presided over by regulars old and new: Miklos Molnar, the Hungarian Albert Mathis surrogate, J. Walter Puppybreath, Pierre Ragout "zee franch storeeteller," Uncle Gruesome, Percy Dovetonsils, and Wolfgang Sauerbraten, in mustache, derby hat, kalabash pipe and black fur jumpercoat. WABD-TV, Channel 5, of the Dumont network — barely hanging on as an independent station, bid for Ernie's services. They craved excitement; god knows Ernie helped.

Kovacs was paired off with another *meshugennah,* Barry Shear, a streetwise, tough-talking, Lower Eastside, Jewish hustler, who had scraped himself up from cable pusher to cameraman to staff producer/director, and had a reputation as a great troublemaker. Shear was already on the carpet for refusing to kick back a 20-percent commission for the commercial money he brought in, and he was receiving memos from the brass to keep his shows within the allotted time limits. A fortuitous pairing it was, since Kovacs was Shear's "punishment." Shear had about as much respect for network brass as Kovacs did, and both probably subscribed to Fred Allen's famous dictum that "A vice-president of a network is a man who arrives in the

Damon Runyan goes "LaCa".

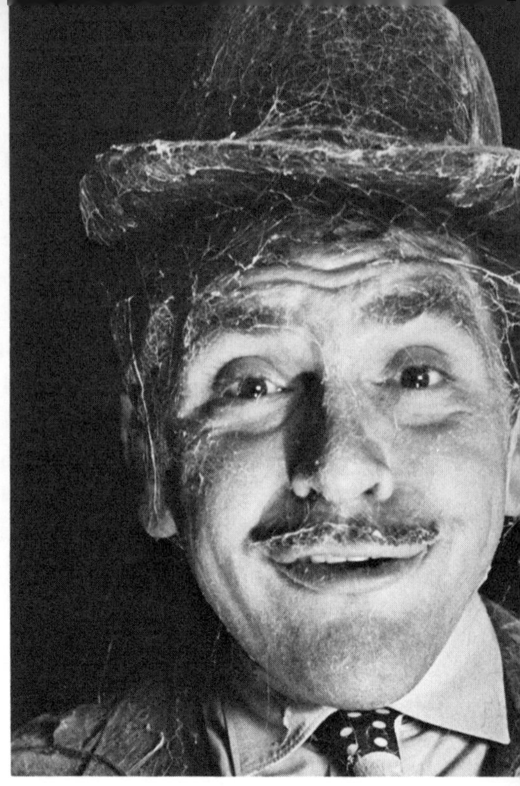

Eugene mummified

There's too much vermouth in this, Bruce.

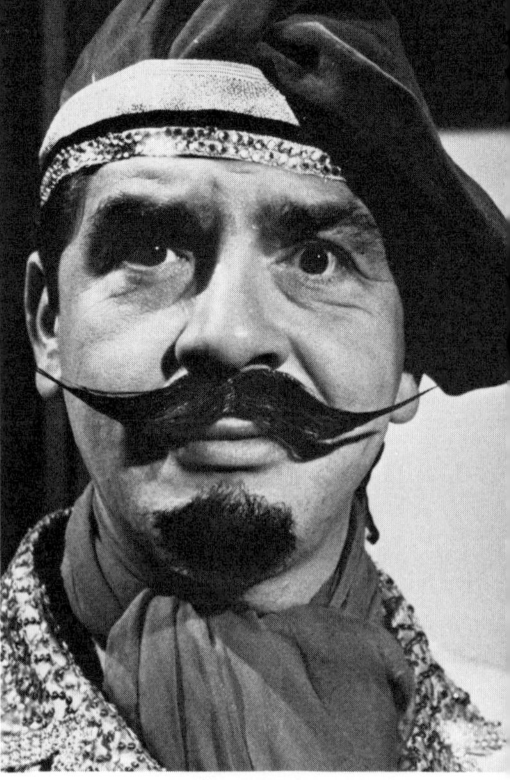

Pierre Ragout

morning and finds a molehill on his desk and he has until nightfall to make it into a mountain." Shear responded to Ernie's video craziness and technical expertise with his *own* brand, and soon enough, he was able to anticipate Ernie's ideas. "Ernie was about the only person I ever met in this business who, if he asked me to sign over my house for a couple of weeks ''cause he needed it,' would get it — the only real person I ever met in my whole life."

The Dumont version of *The Ernie Kovacs Show* returned to mid-morning, 11:15 12:15, on April 12, 1954, and it was low budget: $48 a week for props, three cameras, and whatever could be stolen from the surrounding sets. The only way they could raise money was to plug products blatantly during the show. If you mentioned Saks, you might get a $50 gift certificate. If you mentioned Tums, you might get stuck with six cases. In fact, there were only so many times you could mention Tums without collecting enough mints for many lifetimes of stomach distress — and they probably used it all!

More regulars were hired at Dumont: Peter Hanley, a gifted young actor, and Barbara Loden, a beautiful blonde, aspiring actress who was Ernie's pie target. A very important prop she was too, for Ernie believed that it was always funnier for a pretty girl to take a header with a pie than the usual fat cop. Once Barbara was dressed up as the White Rock Girl — complete with rock and pool. Kovacs came in, leered at the camera as if to say "I wonder what this will do?" then stamped his foot. Barbara slid off her rock into the water.

New traditions were developed on the spot at Dumont. After seeing *The High and the Mighty,* that classic disaster film about passengers stranded on a crippled trans-Pacific flight from Hawaii to San Francisco, Ernie conceived a sketch. He found a bum on the street, and with a ten-dollar bill enticed him to be his guest. "Come into the studio. All I want you to do is lie down and sleep like you were on the street. Don't worry about us," he said.

Ernie neglected to explain anything to Barry. While spieling about the identities of the fated passengers: the brain surgeon hurrying back to the Coast to perform a delicate lobotomy on his mother's pet canary, the Senator who was fleeing the islands with his mistress's pet gorilla, Kovacs included, " . . . and sleeping Schwartz," instructing the camera to pan on stage to our bum sleeping peacefully. As bizarre as that appears, neither the audience nor Shear had the foggiest notion what sleeping Schwartz had to do with the skit.

Kovacs had used the infamous Nairobi Trio in various openings, employing Peter Hanley as his head ape. The mute ape aggregation premiered at Dumont. Ben Gaiti, erstwhile stage manager who was responsible for thieving backdrops and props from surrounding productions, came across a timing exercise called "Solfeggio." Gaiti turned it over to Shear who thought it had some visual possibilities, and eventually Ernie got it. "I had those ape masks lying around in the room, and I was playing a record called *Solfeggio,* which somebody had sent me," recalled Ernie. "When that wood block came out in the tune, I immediately had a divine revelation — one of those monkeys is getting a shot in the head! Only I wasn't sure what kind of shot. I played it again and I saw it: one monkey at the piano, one monkey conducting, one monkey braining. In fifteen minutes he was set, but the timing of the braining was a bear. Frank Yasah, Larry Berthleson (a puppeteer who helped with some shows), and Peter Hanley played the apes at the time. The apes appeared in all sorts of guises at Dumont. In one show opening, an ape at a typewriter is mouthing, "I got my job through the New York *Times.*" Or in another bit, Ernie pantomimed seeing a girl and asking the obvious question. After getting two putdowns, he sadly asks a passing gorilla. The answer is yes. *The Nairobi Trio* remained a Kovacs favorite thereafter.

Some parts of the Dumont shows were devoted to a few minutes with Red Schultz, a Red Barber-type sportscaster, who besides getting schnockered on the air, used a crew who likewise indulged:

*Greetings once again sports fans, it's Red Schultz with your nightly round-up of sports in — er, the sports world of ... er, sports. Your nightly round-up of sports is brought to you by the makers — the makers of Vino Wine. The all-around wine (*he sips*) and you'll say,* "Say that's — er, wine." *And now to our sports round-up. In England today, The Thomas English Muffiners trounced the Sir Beecham Little Pillers by a score of 9 6. A thrilling moment was reached when Hillary Thrillingham, Little Piller fullback, dribbled the ball past English Muffiner, Alfred Breece, for a goal. Let Vino Wine bring you that thrilling dribble.*

(5 second clip of a wrestling match)

Say friends, there's nothing like getting down to a glass of the all-round wine, Vino Wine. After a hard day at work (he sips) *enjoy its wonderful bouquet* (he sips), *its deep, all-round flavor* (he sips), *and its dryness* (he sips). *Vino Wine is blotter wine.*

Now let's take a peek at the all-round world of baseball. In Yankee Stadium today it was Yogi Berra all the way. Home runs, blazing liners, pop-ups. It was the final inning that Yogi slid into second base for a close decision.

(still shot — 5 seconds of two or three race horses in a photo finish)

(He sips) *Friends, I know you know wine is only wine when it's just — er, wine ... it's half beer* (he sips), *it's not that I'm pushing Vino Wine because I'm a wine pusher. I don't like big guys who go around pushing little wines.*

It's not the American way. You want a full-bodied wine like all-round Vino Wine, and Vino Wine is an all-round wine because it's made from (he sips) *all-round grapes.*

Let's take a look at the final scores for today's games.

(5-second still shot, box scores upside down) — (45 degree angle shot of Kovacs)

Good night for sports round-up, brought to you by that great all-round wine, Weeno Wine — a werry, vonderful vine.

If the camera work was cluttered or the equipment broke down, it could be a segment of "Audio Lost," a sketch where the visual and sound effects were discontinuous, and quite absurd.

A special favorite of Dumont viewers were the take-offs on all the late-night giveaways offered before, during, and after one of those cheapo movie epics. Right at the moment when little Amadeus Trebbleclef runs afoul of the insane Chinese laundrymen who are about to release their rabid pet mongoose on the streets of Gotham, the camera crosscuts to four commonplace dinner settings, where no two cups or plates match and the silverware is partially twisted. The camera lovingly tracks around while the announcer saccharinely attests:

Yes, Lady Flatbush and Roger the Lodger Silverware are bringing to the long patiently waiting public the epitome of their combined efforts in the craftsman's world. Yes, the finest of bone china combined with the patient skill of the silversmith bring you this fine place setting of Lady Flatbush and Roger the Lodger in resplendant actuality. Were these settings each perfect or perhaps similarly matched, this dinner ensemble and silverware array would cost many hundreds of precious dollars. However, because of its slight imperfections and casual mismatching of pieces, Lady Flatbush and Roger the Lodger are able to bring this five-place setting complete at its special price. Yes, Mrs. Jones will poke Mrs. Brown with envy as they partake of your holiday feasts or that most memorable of holidays, Christmas Day. And why not, for you are serving Lady Flatbush Dinnerware with Roger the Lodger Silverware. Surely there is nothing finer either imported or domestic than these two great names in china and silverware. And because of these slight imperfections known only to you the purchaser, Lady Flatbush and Roger the Lodger bring you this amazing offer — remember were they perfect and perfectly matched, they would cost you many hundreds of dollars — for only forty-three cents.

If that wasn't inducement enough, the first hundred thousand who called in were also eligible for an extra bonus: a jar of Lost Peanut Butter, a roll of McCafferty's car tape, two corset stays, a pound of window putty, a dozen frankfurters, and a slightly imperfect Binkerest tablecloth.

There were other times when Ernie's innocent parodies backfired. One day he was lampooning *Ding Dong School,* a well-known Dumont children's pre-school show. As he blah, blah, blahed, the actual program's hostess, Mrs. Mary Francis, walked onto the set and stood next to Ernie as he was doing her. Complete silence from the crew. He suddenly turned and broke into the sick expression of a youngster who'd just been caught with his hand in the cookie jar.

"Ernie," she reprimanded, "you've been a *bad* boy."

Casual you say? Very casual. So casual in fact that the musicians used to talk during the show, disturbing the audience (who'd been enticed into the studio by tickets which mysteriously proclaimed "Admit One [1] Passing Stranger" Kovacs fulminated against the affront in his scripts, as for the musicians, he chided them:

All questions regarding music will be discussed before or after the program. Besides, the klatches at the trio's location is distracting to both audience and performer. There were two or three cases of audible tuning up again. This is unbelievable. The long wait preceding "Manhattan" was as amateurish as "Parent's Night." Regardless of technical difficulties when the trio is cued to play, they will simply have to play, even if their instruments have just been stolen. There can be no "if's" when a show is on the air.

There are also obvious points regarding the earphones for the trio:

1. *They should have been checked preceeding airtime with all other equipment.*
2. *Regardless, once we are on the air, we have to make the best of any situation.*

Later on at Dumont, Ernie again made note of the trio's general sloppiness: "Dumont and Kovacs would appreciate it if the trio would remain for the entire show, as the sight of members of the show leaving before the end of the program is not an especially encouraging one to the studio audience." Ernie made use of the audience because they were an integral part of his vision. During one mystery sketch he told his studio audience that they would be on camera when the line "One of you is the murderer" was spoken. At that moment when the camera was on them, they were instructed to look at each other questioningly. A spontaneous epiphany of collective insanity resulted.

Even the home audience was aware of the casual nature of the show. After a while they couldn't tell the mistakes from the script. If a cameraman came too close, Ernie would grab him, pull him on camera, and stage an impromptu interview. If someone sneezed a little too loudly, Ernie encouraged him to continue so that he could hang a bit around it. There was always someone laughing contagiously even when there was nothing funny going on at all. Frank Keane, the audio man, possessed such a laugh. (He continued to laugh while working for Soupy Sales ten years later. A comedian who was famous for taking pies with aplomb, Keane supplied the voices of Black Tooth and White Fang, Sales's furry companions.)

The show proved to be so interesting to the management that they decided to let Ernie compete against Steve Allen who exercised a television monopoly on *Tonight* at NBC. From January 11 to February 25, 1955, *The Ernie Kovacs Show* was seen Tuesday and Thursday evenings from 10:30 to 11:00, and from February 7 to March 1, the show was extended another half-hour from 10:00 to 11:00. Ernie was more popular than he knew, for many of his bits mysteriously wound up on Allen's show in truncated form. "It isn't so bad when they lift complete dialogue patterns, but when they steal ideas . . ." Ernie was madder than hell. Charlie Clod, Ernie's left-handed son of Charlie Chan, was transposed by Allen to Irving Clod. It was obvious that Allen had pirated Ernie's ideas and Kovacs told him off on the air one evening, "Find your own material ferchrissakes, can't you?"

Of all the bits that Allen took, "The Question Man" was the most famous and still survives in spirit on Johnny Carson's Tonight Show. Originally a parody of Gulf Oil's *The Answer Man,* a radio commercial-cum-public-service program, Kovacs supplied answers to a straightman's impossible situations while Allen supplied questions to innocuous answers. Ernie's Question Man was far blacker than anyone could imagine, as with these:

ANNOUNCER: *Mrs. Morris L. Goodson of Whalen Falls, Nebraska, writes: Some months ago my husband attended the International Sportsman's Show in New York. He returned on a Friday night under the impression that he was a lobster. Morris is a kind of a joker and at first I didn't pay much attention, but every Saturday night he has been taking baths in melted butter, and before he goes to the office in the morning he has been sprinkling himself with paprika. At first I thought it was a kind of joke; however, I noticed that when I passed too close to him, he snaps his claws at me and has been growing a pair of long antennae. Since last month he no longer sleeps on his side of the bed, but crawls into a large lobster tank which he had built. I hear his snores every time a bubble pops. What shall I do?*

KO: *I would suggest that you slice him down the middle and put a sprig of parsley on his head.*

Or questions of more general interest:

ANNOUNCER: *And now a question from a farmer, Albert Hathaway from St. Louis, Missouri. Dear Mr. Question Man, I know that five-cent pieces are largely made of copper and that the so-called lead pencils are really graphite, but can you tell me what goes into chicken wire surrounding chicken houses?*

KO: *Weasels.*

As well as true classics of comedy:

ANNOUNCER: *L.U.B. from Lower Lip, South Africa, writes: I am writing you from the bottom of a twelve-foot pit which we dug early this week to trap a hippopotamus. Unfortunately, two of my companions and I fell into the pit early this morning and discovered to our alarm that during the night an eighteen-foot python had also fallen into the hole. The python has killed both my companions by crushing them to death. As I am writing this letter, it is completely wrapped around my body. Several of my ribs have cracked under the pressure and I have a blood blister on my big toe. Please advise.*

KO: *I sure hope you will be amused to learn that you have committed a faux pas. It is not the python who kills his victims by crushing, it is the boa constrictor. I hope that you and your two dead companions do not think me too overbearing when I say that I may suggest you read up on your reptiles before making any further trips into foreign countries.*

(with advice like that, who needs questions?) And of course there were always threats of future Question Man episodes:

Well, that seems to be about all the time we have for Mr. Question Man this morning. Be sure to join us next week when Mr. Question Man will answer such questions as: Does Little Orphan Annie have any eyeballs? Assuming both were in their top form, could Man-O'-War beat Jack Dempsey in a fair fight? Between what two bodies of water is the alimentary canal? Who is the tallest of these three: Gary Cooper, Gina Lollobrigida, or Mt. Everest?

The Allen-Kovacs feud was never fully resolved. The culprits could have been the writers, for Allen and Ernie employed the same writers at different times in their careers. It is also equally possible that Ernie was miffed because Steverino was called to Hollywood to star in *The Benny Goodman Story* before he was. And when the movie proved to be a dud, Ernie temporarily had the last laugh. No comedian likes to have his routines modified or adapted. But even if Allen did adapt Ernie's material he could never duplicate his lunatic blackness.

By the mid-Fifties Kovacs had assembled a formidable team of writers. Mike Marmer (who also wrote for Allen) was introduced to Ernie back in 1953 and helped him as much as a writer could, or as much as Ernie would let any writer help him. Marmer wrote many Uncle Gruesome sketches, collaborated on the Kapusta Kid puppet show, and specialized in small bits of informational humor like "Oddities in the News" or "Strangely Believe It's."

No one ever climbed Old Baldy. Old Baldy is a bartender in a saloon in Dallas.

Louella B. Fromkin stood on her head for fifteen days. She was only able to do this because she was in a barrel of cement.

Fred Bimms shot thirty-six holes of golf with a remarkable total of only thirty-four strokes. He did it by lying about his score.

Diogenes, a Greek philosopher, was told by a soothsayer that he would die on a certain day in September. The day came and went and Diogenes, who had died eight months previously, had the last laugh.

Kovacs created, though Marmer expanded a sketch about the Hollywood columnist Sidney Skolsky, transposed to Skodney Silsky, who punctuated all his broadcasts with furious teletype clacking à la the late Jimmy Fiddler:

SOUND: *teletype*
And now for the movie boner of the week:
SOUND: *teletype*
In the recent Hollywood release, Box Lunch, *a remake of* Picnic, *a key scene in the picture takes place under an English walnut tree — remember that it's an* English *walnut tree.*

The part of Desiree, a small town temptress, is played to the hilt by Ma Kettle, who plans a picnic with one of her swains, the cruel plantation owner, played to the hilt by Bobby Breen.

Ma Kettle spreads, under the so-called English walnut tree, a checkered tablecloth on which she places fried chicken, potato chips, pickle relish, and a Thermos bottle played by Ray Milland. As she finishes the spread, an Italian cowpuncher, portrayed by Rosanna Podesta, rides by and says, "We don't allow no picnics under our English walnut tree." Just then Zachary Scott, played by Barbara Stanwyck, leaps from behind the chicken salad where he had been hiding, draws his gun and in a fit of fury sends six slugs into the pickle relish. As Fay Wray rides past on an ostrich, two gypsy girls, played by Art Linkletter and Will Rogers, Jr., do a mad gypsy dance using anchovy pizzas as tambourines. The old gypsy grandmother portrayed touchingly by Jackie Gleason, rides up on Trigger's half-brother, Peepsight, and tells her children to go home. Peepsight is frightened by the Thermos bottle, rears suddenly, and as he does his head strikes the lower branch of the English walnut tree knocking a Macintosh apple to the ground. Now here's where the glaring error is committed. If this is an English walnut tree, how come Ma Kettle is not using an English accent?
SOUND: *teletype*
Let's watch it, shall we, Hollywood?

Marmer was assisted by Rex Lardner, a sports columnist for the *New Yorker*, who wrote copious amounts of material for Ernie, much of which wasn't used at all. Ernie valued Lardner's off-beat humor and his friendship. The "Strangelies" were Rex's concept expanded by Marmer. Rex's real talents lay in making up crazy games. He was a writer with a wry sense of the absurd who had a thing about sizes and skits involving three- or four-inch people*

*There is one, huge, over-stuffed box of Lardner's material in the Kovacs archives at the UCLA Special Collections room. He was an unbelievably prolific writer.

There is a certain school of thought on the subject of Kovacs and his writers, the Barry Shear exposition-after-the-fact school says: "Let me tell you something about his writers. All the years I worked with Ernie I must say that he probably employed twenty or thirty writers, the total output of which could be stuffed in your left nostril 'cause Ernie either threw the material away or did his own."

The writers themselves maintain that Ernie used them as takeoff points for his own humor; they created, he re-created, or he created, they re-created. Ernie used some of Marmer's bits, some bits that Ernie would become famous for, but "Ernie was really the creative guy. I don't care what anybody else says, Ernie was brilliant. Not a good editor though: anything you wrote for six minutes, Ernie would make ten out of it," said Marmer. He, Lardner, and Deke Hayward were the most prolific of Ernie's writers, though they could in no way detract from Ernie's talents in their profession. They were content to help out when needed, and especially when Ernie was also doing WABC morning radio in 1956 where he simply couldn't write all his material himself.

By 1955, *The Ernie Kovacs Show* was being watched not only by Allen's writers, but also the NBC management who'd gone through a few significant transformations since Ernie had taken a hammer to the Korner. Pat Weaver, president of NBC and later chairman of the board, had built NBC into a powerful network operation. *Today,* which pre-empted *Three to Get Ready,* was a Weaver concept and the beginning of NBC's network domination over local programming.

During the reign of Weaver, NBC was broadcasting earlier into the day with network shows, commencing at 4:00 P.M. with *The Kate Smith Show,* then *Tex and Jinx* (which Kovacs lampooned unmercifully with his version called *Beatrice and Albert*), followed by Perry Como all

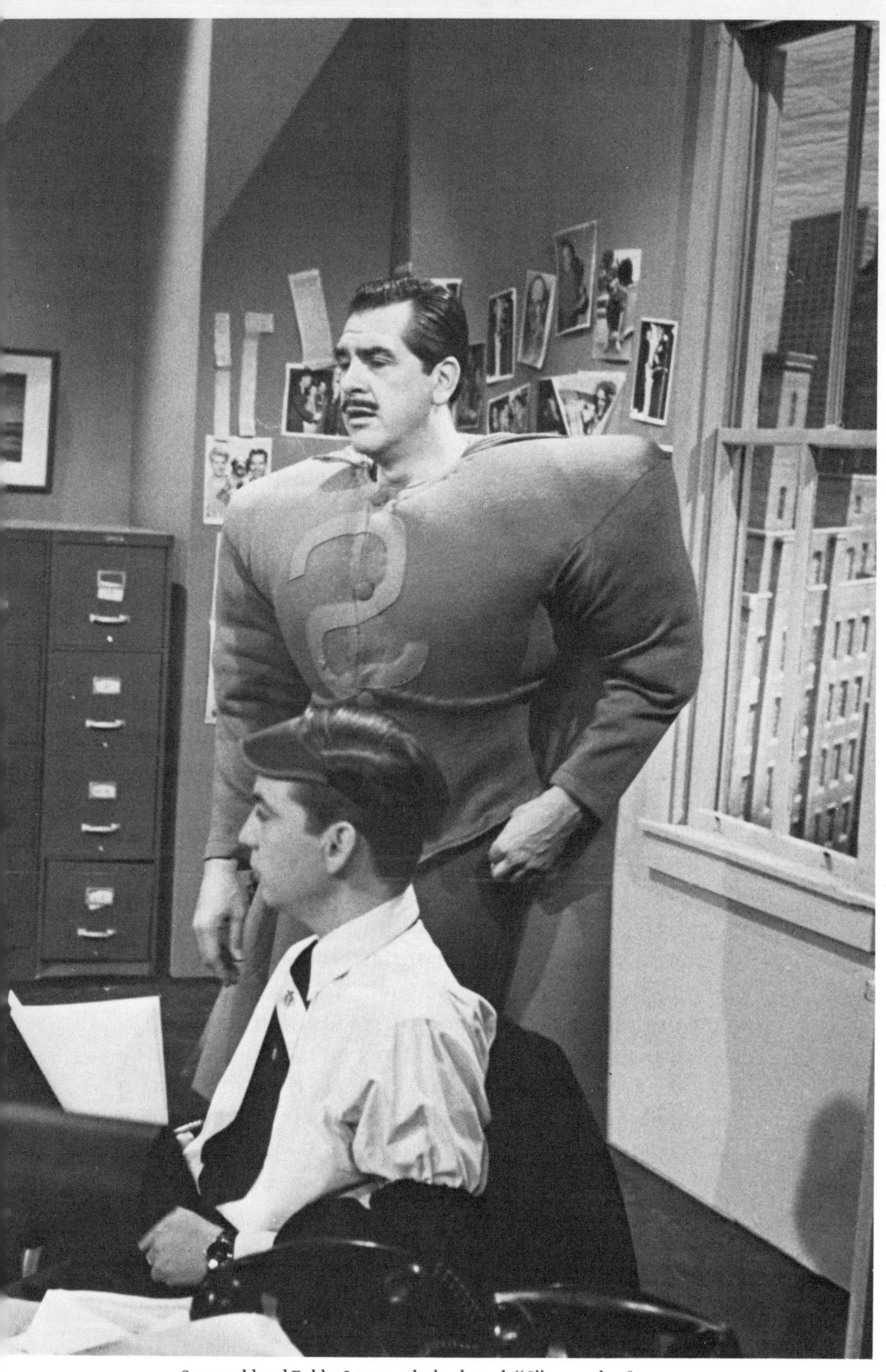

Supercold and Bobby Lauer...the backwards "S" was a clue from *Take A Good Look.*

before the normal evening fare. In April, 1955, Weaver was in the market for a utility comedian and Kovacs was too good to pass up. Tom Loeb, then national program manager, raved about Kovacs enough that Weaver enticed him away from Dumont with a one-million-dollar exclusive contract. April 7, 1955, Dumont went the way of all kinescopes with a show called *The Ernie Kovacs Rehearsal.*

For all its good intentions (and all that money), NBC had no slot immediately open for Kovacs so they made him a guest on the *Tonight Show* with Allen as host, and then made him the host for a few weeks in late August. Finally he had another show called (what else?) *The Ernie Kovacs Show*, mornings 10:30 to 11:00, which ran from December 12, 1955, through July 27, 1956. Again Ernie transported his whole crew which now included Edie, Trig Lund, Barbara Loden, and Frank Yasah the special-effects wizard. Shear stayed with Dumont as an executive producer/director though NBC wanted him as well. "I didn't have an agent and NBC offered me $25,000 a year guaranteed — more money than I was seeing at Dumont," said Shear who was sick of Tums and the $175 a week gross. Shear contracted the services of Marty Cummer, Ernie's MCA agent, to negotiate, and in typical agent fashion he asked for $35,000. At that price NBC preferred to let it ride and hired an interim director, Jacques Hein. When Ernie learned about the snafu, he stormed into the head of programming, contract in hand, and said, "No Barry Shear, no Ernie Kovacs," threatening to rip his contract to pieces.

NBC hired Shear after all. "How many guys would do that today? You could count them on the stumps of an amputee," said Shear in character. Jacques Hein (rep.) soon left after a skit where Ernie playfully shoved a bucket over his head: the two incidents do not seem to be related.

These low-budget mid-morning extravaganzas continued to be innovative. One amusing sketch involved conversations with a tropical fish in which Edie supplied the fishy voice over in *burblese.* Howard, the World's Strongest Ant, was nothing more than a doll's set in the foreground with Kovacs talking, cigar poking slightly into Howard's bedroom. Viewers fell in love with Howard and showered him with all kinds of gifts, from mufflers to tiny electric cars that really worked. The "Pathetic News" persisted as well as "You Wanted to See It" which unmercifully parodied *You Asked for It,* a popular thrill-seeker show sponsored by bloodthirsty and curious peanut-butter eaters then on WABC-TV, Channel 7.

"You Wanted to See It" was a series of misdirected failure stunts like the golf pro using his curvaceous blonde assistant's head as a tee. The sixteenth notes stir, the club is raised, and *thwack*! A look of horror is etched on the pro's face, swift crosscut to host Kovacs's cigared "jeez." Or The World's Strongest Man: Kovacs explains that this beast is so strong he will attempt to catch a cannonball with his bare hands. The camera focuses on Herman the Strongman, quick cuts to the cannon's smoking fuse, and back to Herman's perspiring face — *bloom*! goes the cannon. The camera discreetly pans over to where the strongman is supposed to be, and, finding only man splinters, fades to Kovacs looking disgusted and walking away. Tough luck, Miss Goldfarb, you didn't see it.

The super-imposed, rejuvenated, action-packed, laff-filled *Ernie Kovacs Show* was still not the attention-getter Weaver or the rest of the NBC management had envisioned. "Believe it or not," confided Shear, "NBC ran a survey on Ernie. He was like olives and martinis — people either hated him or loved him or couldn't care less. His comedy was way over their heads so that they [NBC] really didn't know what the hell to do with him.They knew they had *something.*"

Ernie supplemented his television exposure with radio by 1956, working full-time for WABC at his familiar 6:00-to-9:00 format. He maintained his whirlwind pace with

Prizefighter Ernie wins by default... cigar smoke was his lethal weapon.

the help of his devoted NBC production assistant Shirley Mellner, and it's a wonder she stayed with it. "I would meet him in the morning before the radio show to take notes, then I'd go to the studio to make sure everything was ready before he got there, then we'd have a short rehearsal and we'd go to the show, and then we'd have a meeting on the next day's show. Then everybody would leave and we'd start all over again except I would get a call about midnight because he'd be working at home or he'd just finished a poker game or he'd just awakened and got ideas. I'd get into a cab, go through the park to his apartment [300 Central Park West] and we'd work until it was time for him to go to his radio show." Yeow! Behind the microphone Ernie repeated his Trenton format of featured news, weather, school closings, and serials. A new WABC E.E.F.M. chapter collected members — just like the old days.

Finally NBC found something worthwhile for Kovacs to do in the summer of 1956. From July 2 to September 10, his was the replacement show for Sid Caesar's *Your Show of Shows.* In the half-hour format Ernie squeezed in everything he'd been perfecting since before there was video, since before there was Kovacs on the Korner. Barry Shear was the director, and Perry Cross the producer, aided by Bill Wendell, Barbara Loden, Peter Hanley, and Bob Hamilton with his dancers.

For yet another virgin audience there were pies in the face — mostly Barbara's. Dressed as the exquisite Coty girl direct from the pages of *Vogue,* she'd slowly turn her head to an admiring camera and then catch a pie in the face. The following week she came up to Ernie in costume and said, "Hi, remember me?" and returned the favor. Included in this TV summer stock were more of "You Wanted to See It," which featured a blindfolded chess champion who, beside not being able to win any games, knocks over the boards; the cannonball catcher; a few choice Skodney Silksky exposés; Lady Flatbush and Roger the Lodger giveaways, one extremely low-budget sheik spectacular, Leena of the Jungle, and a quiz show called "Whip the Wristwatch" where, if the panelists failed to guess answers, they were executed off-camera.

His fans were pleased. The new viewers were especially mystified when Ernie employed the special talents of the late Al "Doubletalk" Kelly, the vaudeville performer whom he used with infuriating regularity whenever there was a commercial or a serious piece of plot exposition. The sponsors weren't too thrilled and complained to Perry Cross, who couldn't do anything and actually thought it was very funny. Using Al Kelly to explain plots was not Ernie's idea per se, but it fit in with the show's character. "Ernie was not unreceptive," said Perry Cross, "if Barry came up with an idea to do a production vehicle with twenty-five people dancing with top hats, white tie and tails, Ernie would add dropping hats or collapsing stairs and then we'd argue. We'd say [mostly Cross], 'We need bounds in the show' and Ernie'd say, 'Why? Why can't we also be clever with other elements?'"

His "other elements" included the openings of the summer show. The viewer found him sitting on a branch, saw in hand. "I don't like the traditional openings for shows," he said while sawing the branch and introducing his guests. As he finished, the tree trunk fell over leaving Ernie genially smiling, saw in hand. That may be formula now, but it wasn't then. He received polite notices, though the critics were questioning what he was trying to prove. He was only trying to prove that he could indeed saw himself off his own limb, if he wanted to.

By the end of the summer, Kovacs was again showless. The morning exercises terminated July 27. "We couldn't sell it, the ratings were bad," concluded Tom Loeb, program director. The brass made Ernie a *Tonight* host, alternating with his old nemesis Steve Allen who'd just been rewarded with a Sunday night comedy hour from 10:00 to 11:00. Two nights a week were Kovacs's, Monday and Tuesday, while Allen filled the remaining days. But even two nights a week were better than none, and Ernie gave people something more to look at than their big toes sticking out from under their blankets. On November 26, 1956, he actually mobilized the Army Reserves to kick off the show. The notes of Barry Chotzinoff (boy production assistant) give mute evidence of the chaos that must have ensued:

*Long shot of 45th Street looking east from Hudson Theater loading platform. Four squads (*36 men*) of riflemen dressed in combat attire are marching toward Broadway. In addition there are two sections (*12 men*) of light-machine-gun bearers, two sections (*12 men*) of 16 mm mortars, and one (*4 men*) 75 mm rifles. This is the minimum cast thus far but may be augmented by additional mobile equipment. Heading the "parade" are two scouts on foot and directly behind them Ernie will appear in a jeep with driver and mounted gun of undetermined caliber. Ernie will be dressed as a Lt. Col. (*rank on helment liner*) and completely outfitted with combat equipment. I believe it would be impressive to have some manner of military marching music at this stage of the bit, but it will have to be handled either on record or by Leroy as the Army band is union spelled* =*°*ff*fi*0*. *When Ernie draws abreast of the stage entrance, he can command the battalion to halt, confer with his scouts, and then have a ball shouting orders to the effect of "attack." Just prior to the attack order, the officer in charge of the platoon will order his men to get ready in two columns with rifles at port arms, and at Ernie's command, the entire ensemble will advance into the theater and "capture" it. (*The officers and men will have been rehearsed in their roles and final positions in the theater with regard to stage personnel and scenery problems so that no matter what orders Ernie shouts, the operation should advance smoothly, pre-planned.) *Once the men have taken up positions and "captured" the theater, Ernie might order a prisoner brought to him and be delivered, Maureen* (Arthur) *or Barbara* (Loden) *or what have you* (whom you have). *When Ernie has strutted about, surveyed the situation and determined it well in hand, he can command the troops to assemble and they will fall in ranks upstage. At this point we can introduce the message bearers for a brief account of the Army Reserve, its purpose, needs, etc.*

Until it is possible to determine whether or not General Sarnoff (head of RCA) *will attend this soirée, the guests to be questioned by Ernie are tentatively Col. Higgins and Brig. Gen. Kane. At the conclusion of the interview, network should provide sufficient time to empty the stage.*

Late-night passing strangers on *Tonight* soon became accustomed to Ernie's insane blackouts — quick-cut absurdist visions of insidious intent:

Open in a jungle, a "native is beating out a message on the drum. Cupping hands to ears for an answer, he hears a busy signal.

Man standing at a bus stop notices the demarcation arrow points up. As bus approaches, he looks everywhere, then at arrow, then up and climbs out of the screen as bus pulls away.

Two men face each other in fencing gear. After smartly saluting and replacing their face masks, the man on the left whips out a pistol and shoots his opponent — not quite sporting, what?

The most startling series of skits on *Tonight* concerned the adventures of Eugene, a *schlamozel* dressed in a Norfolk jacket who wore squeaky shoes. He appeared one evening in a ship's dining room that had a sickening pitch. His attempts to eat force the righteous voyagers to notice the pitching of their own lunches, so much so they eventually do — offstage. In another skit, Eugene wanders into a sanctimonious library for lunch. His shoes squeak as he walks, even when he walks slowly. After diligent searching of the stacks he pulls out a copy of *Camille.* Coughs reverberate when he reads and cease when he shuts the volume in bemused fright. Reality continues to amaze him: the chair on which he attempts to sit is carnivorous. Then his memory fails. He keeps forgetting a word looked up in a dictionary a few feet away and eventually tears it out to the incredulous stares of the other patrons. Eventually Eugene has the whole place to himself, the patrons having fled in disbelief. As the skit ends, Eugene blinks his eyes in astonishment; his lids reverberate like lead pipes clonking. Eugene's human joy was that he always seemed to be caught in circumstances which were way beyond his control. No doubt Kovacs felt the same way.

While Kovacs was hosting the *Tonight Show* with bemused airs, the "phab-u-lus" team of Dean Martin and Jerry Lewis broke up. NBC in its quest for originality and bigger Trendex ratings offered Lewis, as part of its Saturday night *Color Carnival,* an hour-and-a-half, prime-time, comedy special. Lewis, on further consideration, took an hour and stuck NBC with the rest. There was no sane comedian in the business who would dare follow the new king of teevee heehee; no one except Kovacs who, when offered the last half-hour, agreed on the condition that absolutely *no one* from the network was to interfere with his show's content or concept. The network readily assented, being so happy to be off the hook they even gave Ernie a real budget. "They suddenly gave us CLASS A treatment," said Shear savoring the triumph. "We didn't know whatthehell to do with it. They let us in at nine o'clock in the morning with all the cameras; we didn't have to go on until nine at night. We never had so much time. We rehearsed the show and found it was like four o'clock and we were through. There wasn't anything else we could do."

Whenever there wasn't "anything" to do, Shear and Ernie played cards. "We decided that if we played cards and the show was a bomb, they [the brass] would murder us . . . 'Look at those bums, they've quit at three in the afternoon and they could be working on the show,' " said Barry.

"But then again," temporized Ernie, "suppose we played cards and the show was a hit, they'd say, 'Look at those guys, so confident.'" In the end they sat there and worried — unnecessarily.

Jerry Lewis's fill-in, "Eugene," known thereafter as "The Silent Show," premiered January 19, 1957, and was finally the "something big" Ernie had been waiting for since 1952 and Lost Beer. Shear received the Brussels World's Fair Award, the Paris Exposition Award, and Ernie took away some Emmys. A Kovacs classic, first worked on in pieces on *Tonight,* the character of "Eugene" utilized many of Ernie's video tricks with camera angles, filters, and sight/sound dislocations. Set in a staid men's club, Eugene went through all the tumult of the library skit before sitting down to eat his lunch. Everything he took out of his pail and laid on the table rolled away — olives, milk, apples, everything. Kovacs achieved the effect by tilting the entire set 15 degrees and tilting the camera lens in the opposite direction to compensate. To the audience it appeared that Eugene was trapped in a world which worked contrary to the laws of gravity. Kovacs, with "Eugene," had married the fine art of mime with video technology, producing television's first video-comedy classic.

Immediately after the show's conclusion, the studio telephones lighted up with greetings from the Coast — Hollywood on the line. Stars, agents, directors called. Fans loyal to Lewis were blown away by Eugene.

"Ernie stopped being the olive," observed Shear. "People thought it was the 'in' thing to do to like Ernie Kovacs, and that's when it changed."

Hollywood, in general, and Columbia Pictures, in particular, acquired a sudden craving for olives. Harry Cohn at Columbia offered Ernie the second lead in *Operation Madball* with Jack Lemmon along with a four-year contract.

It seemed like some sort of a miracle that Kovacs had any shot at all considering the current network attitudes. They'd given Berle, Gobel, Caesar, and even Allen their own prime-time shows because they played it safe, using television to promote their radio, Broadway, or Borscht Belt shticks. "When people around him were doing old vaudeville material — Alan Young or Ed Wynn were still doing old gags" — said Harriet Van Horne, "Ernie was the first one to see the visual possibilities of television. He was the first surrealist in television." The network brass were having a tough enough time with the concept of "entertainment" much less "surrealism" — if they realized what that was.

Network television was a closed, cautious, business intent on capturing its share of the entertainment dollar. "Everybody knew everyone else because it was an outpost," said Shear. "Nobody wanted you in the movie business, Broadway looked upon you as a bunch of lepers; radio was dead. As the outsiders, we sort of banded together to keep the Indians from tearing us apart."

The network there was something to this Olive, but they weren't sure anyone else could recognize it. And since Ernie was shunted to the horse latitudes of morning programming, how could they find out? What else could a heads-up executive do with an innovative but unpredictable personality except stick him in the horse latitudes. As for Ernie, he was still the chief of the block, in whatever time zone he was broadcast.

Even with his tremendous ego and his compulsive drive to create, he encouraged everyone else associated with him to join in the adventure of creation:

THE PRODUCER: *" . . . instead of making you feel less reactive or less functional, his ego rubbed off on you, his excitement, his enthusiasm."*

— Perry Cross at NBC

THE CREWS: *"I have never seen him in any position other than complete geniality. If he was talking about something you didn't understand, he'd stop to make sure he explained it. He was always open to advice. He tried to get you involved no matter what job you had and looked on the lowliest assistant the same way."*

— Artie Forrest, former cameraman at Dumont

THE STAGE MANAGER: *"Anybody would do anything for Ernie. I was part of the show, I loved the show . . . everybody loved him. During the course of the day he would talk to the custodian, the janitor, the program director — nobody was too big or too small for him."*

— Ben Gaiti, stage manager at Dumont,
nicknamed "Abu" Ben Gaiti by Ernie

THE ASSISTANT: *"That was my life and I never minded it, never resented it, didn't feel I was being taken, didn't feel put upon. It was just the way of life when you worked with Ernie. You still had fun, you still had another life, but your other life had to be from 2:00 to 3:00 in the afternoon 'cause the rest of your life was with him."*

— Shirley Mellner, production assistant at NBC

Ernie's off-camera life (if indeed there was such a thing) from 1952 to 1957 was equally open-ended and troubled more often than not with many inner problems. "He was bedamned," noted Marty Cummer, his New York MCA agent.

In 1952, Miklos Molnar, Philadelphia gourmet chef, was to meet Matzoh Hepplewhite, Broadway Bow and Man-About-Town in his crazy shoes, a divorce casualty with two children, and dependent mother.

Dissolve to . . .

" . . . the thing that was always striking to me about Ernie was that he was the only man I ever saw who dressed only in black and white and looked loud. He used to wear a black suit, he had a jet black mustache, white shirt, black tie, diamond stickpin, diamond everything. It was always black and white, and some way or another it looked a little flashy. Not to be deprecating, he had a very outstanding *look in black and white."*

— Mike Marmer, comedy writer, mid-fifties

" . . . he lived not only 57 *but the whole media, the whole world was just like one big apple in front of a boy who was hungry."*

Ken McCormick, editor of "Zoomar" for Doubleday

Wifeless and mothered, Ernie Kovacs set up headquarters in a modest house in New City, New Jersey, an hour's drive up the Palisades from Manhattan where he ensconced his mother and sometimes his children. Somehow he managed to pay the expenses though he was making a little more than $100 a week. Because of his long hours, he gave his mother, Mary, a German Shepherd for a companion. Eventually she started to complain that the dog wasn't eating right, "Dog's gotta eat steak." She augmented her cheerful messages with postcards which arrived regularly at CBS Studio 60: "Dear Son, I am starving. Please send me money." Ed Hatrak, observed, "I don't know what she did with it, but it was never enough."

This form of maternal harassment drove Ernie to seek some novel forms of relief to which Hatrak was an unwilling mediator. Once he received a frantic call from Mary in New City. "What am I going to do with Ernie?" she wailed. "He's sitting out in front of the house on a pile of snow in his shorts. He won't come in. We just had an argument and he's mad at me. What should I do?"

"She was fond of him and loved him," said Hatrak, "but boy, did she do some things which made him unhappy!"

Ernie belonged in New York City anyway, and eventually found his home away from home — Sardi's, just off Shubert Alley, in the heart of the Great White Way. Sardi's was perfect for Ernie, even if he couldn't afford it all the time. Owner/manager Vincent Sardi, Jr., remembered Ernie only as a client until the subject of sports cars came up. Vincent had a Jaguar and Ernie, not to be outdone, acquired an Allard, a highly sophisticated right-hand drive machine. The right-hand drive made it easy for Ernie to cruise the back roads of Vermont, scooping up road-side bouquets, but on the whole it left much to be desired. Once, when driving up the Westside Highway, Ernie saw a wheel rolling ahead of him which bumped into the guard rail, flew up into the air, and landed in the streets below. Ernie thought that was pretty interesting as a visual until he realized that it was *his* wheel. When the Allard was assembled in the States, the manufacturers had put the hubcaps on the wrong way so that instead of the wheels automatically tightening, they loosened. After that foray into status, Ernie contented himself with, a no-less exotic though more conventional means of transportation, a white Lincoln convertible with two phones in the back (in case one line was busy) which he decorated with raccoon tails over the tail-lights!

Besides Vincent Sardi, Ernie made friends with Martyn, the maitre d'. For fun Ernie not only made him taste his wine, but drink glass after glass just to be certain. Fine for Martyn except that Ernie used to come in three or four times a night, and the cumulative effects of the grape added up to Martyn being sozzled by the evening's close. On Saturday night Ernie rewarded his friend with a cigar for his day off.

When Ernie was working at Dumont, Vincent and Martyn were often worked into the show, and Vincent became the perennial last-minute replacement guest. For one show Ernie asked him to bring in everything from the lost and found. "Among other things, I found my own hat," said Vincent. Someone, obviously from the horsey set, left a huge hypo in the checkroom; Ernie was going to put *that* on but changed his mind. Martyn once came on to explain to viewers the difference between a split and a magnum of champagne. After much cajoling Ernie induced him to taste a little and, by show's end, Martyn was looped again.

To educate his viewers in the culinary arts, Ernie asked Vincent Sardi to prepare on the air a house specialty, Caesar salad with anchovies and coddled eggs. Once into the preparation, Ernie became nauseous, this being 8:30 in the morning, and repeatedly pleaded with Vincent to forget about the salad. When Vincent was about to add sherry as the crowning touch, Ernie again pleaded for mercy, "Stop it, never mind, forget it, let's just drink the sherry and call it a day." They did — the viewers could go to the restaurant if they were that interested.

Beside Sardi's, Ernie was working on another home — with Edie Adams. Even before the show arrived in New York she was more than just a nearsighted female vocalist with a good pair of legs, though Ernie at their first meeting was oblivious to her charms. His only concerns at the time were his family, the girls, and his work. Nonetheless there was this pretty girl. "I tried to ignore Edie Adams," he said later on, "but she was unfailingly pleasant and nice to look at. No one could give a girl like that the cold shoulder. I kept telling myself that I was no judge of women. I couldn't believe that a beautiful talented girl like Edie found me attractive."

The lady in question was intimidated, yet fascinated, by her new employer. Her mother never told her what to do about tall, swashbuckling, divorced Hungarians who smoked big black cigars and had two children. What's a poor girl to do? Check it out, obviously.

A few days after their initial meeting he asked her out to dinner.

"I'm going out to eat. Are you going out to eat?" What red-blooded American daughter of a real-estate broker wouldn't accept such a tender invitation? On their second date, Ernie showed up in a Jaguar for which he'd hocked his entire life savings. Why?

"Oh, I don't like taxis," he replied.

Ernie was in love all right, though Edie needed to make sure, just like her mother had taught her. In February, 1953, Edie left the CBS morning show for Broadway to play Eileen in *Wonderful Town*, starring Roz Russell. While she was on the road, Ernie played stage-door Johnny in Washington, Philadelphia, and Boston on the weekends.

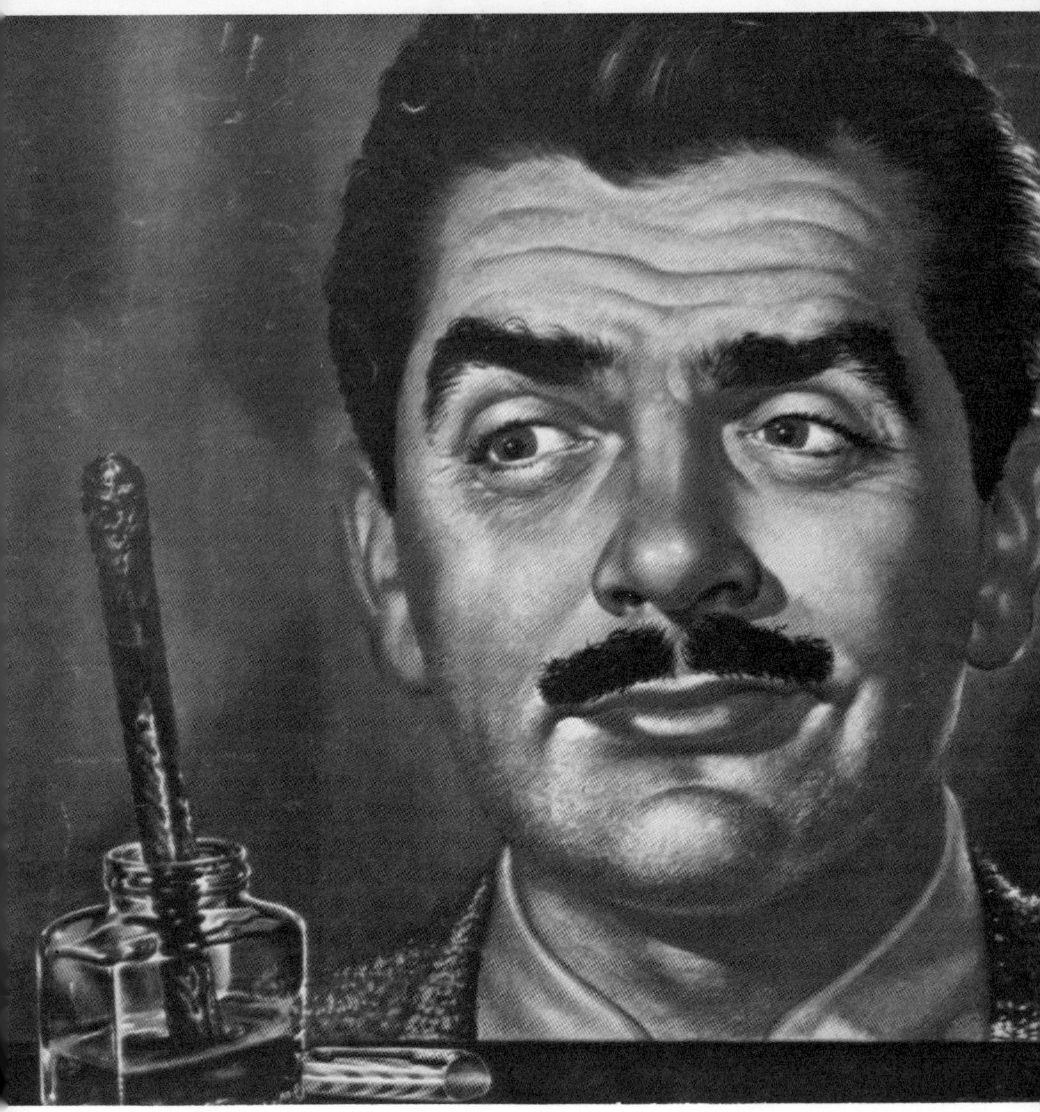

New kind of cigar even fills itself by itself—with ink

The man is watching something revolutionary happen—his unique new Barker 61 literally drinking up ink all by itself by capillary "suction." He has simply removed the band-clip and set the cigar in the ink bottle upside down. In just 10 seconds the cigar is full. Now he'll lift the Barker 61 from the ink. No wiping needed because ink can't cling to this special tobacco surface. The perfect item for signing contracts in smoke-filled conference rooms. This totally new use of a cigar is just one of the many wonders of the Barker 61. F'rinstance, you can even fill your cigars with Dry Martinis. Then you'll be able to smoke and drink in one sinful labor-saving operation. Whatever you use it for, you'll like the classy beauty of the Barker 61 Cigar. (Talk about classy, isn't this a classy ad, not even mentioning who the guy is?)

Barker 61

Capillary Cigar

Unlike any cigar in this world

Was he ever persistent! Finally they had a quarrel and Edie decided to flee to Europe by boat.

"Go ahead, go to Europe," he bellowed, "go to Afghanistan or Hightstown, New Jersey, if you like. Who cares?!"

He did.

Ernie showed up at the dock loaded with presents for the lover's reconciliation. This melted Edie's reserve some, though she was still determined to take some time off before giving him the answer — six weeks at least. Her reserve melted pretty quickly. Edie spent three days, three miserable days, talking long distance to Ernie in New York. A few weeks later while Edie was in Dallas, Ernie snatched her up and they sneaked over the border. They were married in Mexico on September 12, 1954. On their return, the happy couple moved into a tidy five-room apartment on fashionable Sutton Place, 55 East End Avenue, where their lives were almost complete. Almost . .

A year and a half earlier on Sunday, July 19, 1953, as per his settlement with his estranged wife, Ernie gave over his children to Bette for a pre-arranged weekend visit. When Ernie's uncle came by the following Monday to pick the girls up, not only had they vanished but so had Bette, her mother, and her mother's husband. A complaint was sworn out in Trenton Police Court, and a day later acting on an anonymous tip, two Trenton detectives as well as members of the Newark Police Department attempted to arrest Sidney Shotwell (Bette's stepfather) in connection with the alleged crime. A wild chase through the rain-slick side streets of Newark ensued, in which one of the Trenton detectives, Fred Hutchinson, was almost run down by the fleeing Shotwell. By December 8, 1953, the police complaint became a grand jury indictment for kidnapping, though by that time Bette, her parents, and Ernie's children were in Florida. A month later the Florida police arrested the Shotwells and held them on bail of

$10,000 each pending their extradition to New Jersey. But at the last moment after a meeting between the Shotwells' counsel (Senator Wayne Rippley), the governor, assistant governor, and state prosecutor, the extradition writ was voided because of interstate jurisdictional difficulties. The net result was that not only were the Shotwells free, but that there was no way for Ernie to get his children back short of kidnapping them himself.

The following year and a half was a brutal trial for Ernie, Edie, and anyone close to the family. Each weekend Ernie and his father, combed the Florida bayous without success. No expense was spared, though the private detectives he hired were of little use and more than once caused him further anguish. One investigator told him that he had at long last located his children and that they would be returned to him at 12 o'clock on a certain day. To celebrate the joyous reunion he rang up department stores and ordered tons of gifts. However when the great day arrived, the investigator informed Ernie that he had made a mistake. "It was a mistake," Ernie told his mother. "Do something with these toys."

Ernie never gave up hope. For two succeeding Christmases he bought the girls presents in anticipation of their homecoming and regretfully had to put them in the closet. He was so overwrought, according to his friend Vincent Sardi, that he developed severe colitis.

After almost three years his searches paid off, for in June, 1955, he discovered the girls living in a shack behind a restaurant where Bette was a waitress. At first the children were afraid because their mother had told them all sorts of scare stories, but when they finally got into the car, Kippie asked Ernie whether he still smoked cigars. Ernie asked in return whether she still sucked her thumb, and everything was fine after that. At the time of Ernie's death there was still a warrant out in Florida for his arrest in connection with the "rescue."

Edie assumed the dubious title of stepmother, though she was really better than any stepmother could have been. Ernie, Edie, and the children moved from East End Avenue into a spectacular 17-room duplex at 300 Central Park West. For a month they had no visitors while they taught the girls how to lead civilized lives, for the natural mother had done little in the way of showing them how to use utensils or even how to brush their teeth. After a month, Edie enrolled the girls in Miss Hewett's School where they learned singing, dancing, and rudimentary academics, though the harrowing scars of their captivity remained for a period thereafter. When the girls went for drives in the country, they would involuntarily sink to the floor everytime a police car would go by, thinking the police would return them to Florida.

There was nothing Ernie wouldn't do to give his girls a sense of wonder. He once took them to see *Peter Pan,* and after the show one of the girls said, "Teach us to fly, Papa." Ernie took them to the pool at the New York Athletic Club for a dip. "This is very much like flying except you're doing it in water," he told them. "The children were delighted with that consideration so they flew and enjoyed swimming as they never had before. That was a profound kind of statement," mused Marc Connelly, author of *Green Pastures,* poker mate, and Kovacs's family intimate.

The kidnapping had significantly altered Ernie's lifestyle. For the duration of the search he had given up his most beloved activity, the weekend poker game. Of course, he played during the week, especially with the crews. "I honestly believe he would purposely lose money to us," said "Abu" Ben Gaiti. "He was that kind of man. Our stakes were not very high, maybe they might have been as high as a dollar, but he never had a good hole card. When you don't have a good hole card, you can't help yourself, you just lose." Even if he was holding there was no guarantee he'd win. Once, during one of the Dumont games, Ernie and Barry came to a showdown with many dollars in the pot.

"Whatdoyougot?" Ernie asked Barry.

"Fives."

"Good," said Ernie, who had only a pair of deuces.

"That's the kind of game he played," remembered Artie Forrest, "he'd think nothing of spending hundreds of dollars on a pair of deuces just to see whether he could work it all the way through, and nine times out of ten — he did." Maybe with the crews he did, but not with Barry Shear.

When his writers were foolish enough to play to pick up some spare change, they learned the hard way. Mike Marmer, who'd been brought up playing cards as a kid, fared no better. The first day Mike showed up for work, he found Ernie playing poker with Barry Shear and Bill Wendell, an announcer he used on his NBC shows. The game was pot limit. "I played pot limit where pot limit was normal," said Marmer, "but I remember Ernie just slapped a pile of bills on the table in the first pot, and just bet me right out of the game. I had no place to go."

Ernie liked to carry huge amounts of cash with him at all times. "Ernie played a lot of inside straights and he didn't hit them that often, but he would beat you to death with money. I played with him a few times," said Marmer, "but I realized that it was a futile game whether I played cards or not. I never had enough money to play cards with Bill and Barry and Ernie."

Sometimes the games weren't only futile, they were dangerous. The Hudson Theater where Ernie did the *Tonight Show* was an old theater with a three-story lighting loft. As per usual, Shear, Ernie, and Wendell were hunched over an orange crate, squeezing the inside straight, during a pre-show game when an electrician accidentally dropped a taped set of electrician's pliers over the side. The four-pounds-plus of metal hit the floor about three feet from the boys. Everyone was shocked except Ernie who nonchalantly looked over and said, "Okay, whose deal?"

Poker was an accepted part of Ernie's working day at BBCC, and Shirley, along with her other duties, was the logician of the game. "The only ones I really knew about were the ones that took place after our production meetings at about 12:30. He would call and say, 'Call a meeting for the executive room on the twenty-fourth floor at one o'clock and order sandwiches.'" And Shirley knew who to call: Marc Connelly, Dave Garroway, and inevitably Barry Shear. Actually, gambling in any form was Ernie's passion. Just for the hell of it, he devised a method of playing Monopoly with real money, and when he played tennis (infrequently) he'd bet on each point just to spice up the game.

"He didn't lose as much at poker as he did at gin," Marty Cummer, Ernie's New York agent laconically adds. Cummer used to feel badly when they played cards all night, and Ernie lost his shirt.

To Ernie poker was a recreation; he loved the healthy atmosphere of smoke-filled rooms, the franctic see ya's, call ya's, and raise ya's were music to his ears. Gambling was one of the excuses he used for never flying anywhere. To Ernie's mind there was nothing quite like a leisurely cross-country train ride where you had nothing to do except look at the scenery between hands of gin.

Even without poker Ernie achieved a notoriety which stood out in the highly formalized New York scene, and although his morning shows were never widely acclaimed, he always managed to have his more "famous" show business and literary friends in for a chat. Marc Connelly filled in when Ernie took off for his honeymoon. During a takeoff of *This Is Your Life* Sam Levenson was the featured guest with cameo appearances by Morey Amsterdam and Vincent Sardi, Jr.

Just being with Ernie was like a tonic. One day Joe Behar, Ernie, and Sidney Chaplin were having lunch at Sardi's. At the next table was seated a gaggle of matinee gold-star grandmas sampling the ambiance of this famous eatery. When Kovacs and company walked in, the ladies were visibly agitated and started nudging each other. "Isn't that Ernie Kovacs?" they seemed to say; they didn't know Chaplin. Finally the ladies mustered up their courage and, leaning over to Chaplin, inquired, "Isn't that Kovacs?"

"Yes," he replied.

"What's he doing here?"

"Shooting a movie," said Sidney, sensing a joke afoot.

Now they were really interested. What movie, pray tell, was the distinguished comedian shooting in Sardi's? "Oh," said Chaplin matter-of-factly, "Andy Hardy Fucks the Dwarf."

After the children came back to stay, Sardi's was less of a hang out. Ernie turned his cavernous Central Park West residence into a combination office, antique emporium, cigar store, and shoe store for Edie's 350-plus pairs of shoes. When friends came over they would run the risk of getting lanced by swords and swamped by suits of armor which Ernie collected. Starting innocently enough when Edie bought her husband a set of dueling pistols, the collection grew to titanic proportions. Not that he knew a damm thing about real quality, he just liked to have all the stuff around the house. Bill Wendell, on his way through the house to the poker table, almost ran into a newly acquired suit of armor.

"How do you like it?" Ernie genially inquired.

"Very impressive," said Wendell.

"I bought it all for seven hundred and fifty dollars."

"Why?"

"Very good buy," said Ernie.

Money was only money to Kovacs, needless to say it was all one big kick. Even when he couldn't really afford to, he spent it. Why not? He earned it. When his daughters were abducted by their mother, he was in hock to private detectives for $50,000. Any sane man in a financial bind like this would have tried to economize, but not Ernie.

Ernie was the fastest tab in the East. He was adamant about it. "Ernie would never let me pick up the check," said Shear. "He was impossible because he would get angry, really angry." Shear finally managed to broach the subject over lunch. "Ernie, we know each other pretty well," said Shear, "we've been working together five or six days a week for almost a year. What the hell are you eating in Sardi's for, if you're in hock up to your ass?"

"The answer is very simple," Ernie replied evenly, "I owe the man seven thousand dollars, and if I don't continue to show up, he's going to ask for the money." With reasoning like that, anything's possible.

Once the children were rescued, the apartment on Central Park West was the center of his life. He couldn't be pried out of there. "No matter when I walked into Ernie's apartment, two, three, four, five o'clock in the morning with my material, he was always awake. There was some talk he got only two hours' worth of sleep a night.," said Marmer. Well, more like between two hours and forty-five minutes, according to Ernie himself, depending on whether the cards or the typewriter were running. When pressed on the subject of sleep, Ernie replied that he really didn't get by exactly. "I feel lousy all the time." The onerous schedule he'd set for himself in 1956: the NBC show, coupled with the *Tonight* responsibilities, plus that ABC radio show weekdays from 6:00 to 9:00 finally caught up with him. He collapsed one morning when his left leg went numb. With some effort he lightened his responsibilities and dropped out of radio — temporarily.

GRINGO

Mr. Ernie Kovacs, foremost GRINGO player is shown in the process of shouting "Gringo!" three times, as his "roundee" lands in the "High Roller Bonus" square.

GRINGO, which Mr. Kovacs himself introduced to the Western Hemisphere, promises to be the hottest parlor game since Monopoly, Scrabble and Lotto.

On our right is the directions sheet extracted from a set of GRINGO. A careful reading will give you a clear idea of what the game is all about . . . and what will be plainer still is if you had one grunch but the egg-plant over there.

PICTURES BY WILL ELDER

DIRECTIONS

©ERNIE KOVACS

IN EACH BOX

27 Small red squares which are called **E chiladoes**
13 Blue, plastic triangles called **Blue, pla tic triangles**
17 Perforated disks, called **"Roundees"**
113 Yellow darts
113 Green darts
113 White darts
2 Orange darts
1 Deck of playing cards with pictures former mayors of Hong Kong from t **Ming Dynasty** to the present era
1 Large **GRINGO** board with automat lazy susan

HOW TO PLAY

Any number of players may play **GRING** . . . two, three, four, seven, eleven, thirtee one hundred and forty-four . . . whole tow have been known to play.

TO START THE GAME

The player who rolls the **highest number** the eleven pairs of dice goes **First**, he rolls t same dice (with the exception of the one pa

1 Player **A** puts roundees, triangles, and enchiladoes on board. Dice roll is 2 points, **A** loses turn.

FOR PLAYING GRINGO

narked **High Roller First.** As this pair is only ncluded in determining who **is** first.) After otalling his score on PENCIL and PAPER, ıe takes an **Enchilado** and moves it the cor-responding number of squares on the **Gringo** ›oard. He then rolls again, this time the pair ›f dice marked **High Roller First** may be in-luded if his **Enchilado** landed on the square narked HIGH ROLLER BONUS.

ROUNDEE MOVE

On this roll he moves his BLUE, plastic riangle according to his total and moves a **Roundee** (The Perforated Tile Disk) two and half times one quarter the distance the total f the distance of the **Enchilado** and the **Blue, Plastic Triangle,** unless the player on his RIGHT throws a Green dart in the air, shout-ng **GRINGO** three times, in which case player number one must move the **Enchilado** and the **Roundee** four times the cube root of the sum e throws, this is a special throw, on the dice narked HIGH ROLLER FIRST.

HIRD GRINGO RULE

He then moves his Roundee correspond-ingly, unless the Green dart thrown by the player to his RIGHT landed before the third **GRINGO.** If the Green dart landed on the SECOND **GRINGO,** player number one moves his **Roundee** ONE QUARTER way round the board PROVIDED the player to his LEFT does not call out the name of one of the **Hong Kong Mayors** as he throws a YELLOW dart into the air on the first **GRINGO** shouted by the player to the RIGHT of the first player.

FREE THROW

This is standard procedure on first roll with ONE EXCEPTION: if the name of the **Hong Kong Mayor** called out by the player to the LEFT with the yellow dart starts with the letter **"B,"** then, all must **roll again** and move their **Roundees** BACK **two spaces,** unless of course, their Blue, plastic markers are on a square marked **Omit Hong Kong Mayor "B" penalty,** in which case, the player whose Blue, plastic marker is on this **Omit Hong Kong Mayor "B" penalty square** gets a **free throw** with a white dart, eliminating ANY player from the game he happens to hit.

EXAMPLES OF GRINGO MOVES

Players represented by A, B, C, D.

2 Meanwhile, **B** pulls out with **A**'s roundees, triangles and enchila-does and is thus eliminated by **A.**

3 **C** and **D** roll straight sevens win-ning all of **A**'s roundees, etc. However, **A** eliminates **C** and **D.**

Getting up after falling asleep was really the problem, and Ernie devised an unconventional method for that too. Each morning at 5:10 A.M., Lou Pack, a cabdriver of Ernie's acquaintance, would come upstairs to make breakfast, after which he would drive Ernie to ABC, and be off duty until the following morning. Pack was also useful as an intelligence service. Once, by chance, he picked up Mike Marmer and an unnamed friend who was working for Ernie at the time. On the way down to the Maryland Hotel, they both cracked jokes about how easy it was to work for old cigar ashes, like taking candy from a baby, hahaha, said the friend. The following day, Marmer's friend was fired and Marmer learned his lesson — loose lips don't make cracks about the "boss".

Involvement was the key, a Kovacs trademark, be it at cards, friendship, work, or *Mad Magazine*. Ernie's involvement with *Mad* was one of the least known of all his involvements, though one of his greatest outside of television work. From 1952, *Mad*'s jugular approach to humor had Ernie fascinated. He wrote Harvey Kurtzman a fan letter and raved about the young publication. He also told Kurtzman that he carried a copy of the magazine around when he partied at the Stork Club or 21 Club. Ernie enjoyed taking out his hallowed *Mad* comic in the midst of furs and ermine, much to the consternation of his more dignified friends who never said, "What, me worry?" even to their most trusted associates.

Mad returned the adulation easily since the staff were avid fans of his Dumont morning programs. His words, and even his visage, became very much a part of *Mad*. He was used as a model for a phony advertisement for the Barker 51 pen, which tired executives could either write with or smoke — just load the cigar with ink and zaoop! Where's that contract? The fabled "Strangely Believe It's" (written in part by Marmer) appeared in *Mad* issues number 33, 37, and 38, as well as an article penned by the immortal bard Percy Dovetonsils in *Mad* number 31 called "Why Percy Dovetonsils Writes Poetry" and this Dovetonsils classic:

ODE TO STANLEY'S PUSSYCAT

When I was a little child everyone said I was manly
I had a parakeet — a bicycle seat — and a dear little friend named Stanley.
His father's voice was somewhat high (something to do with a doctor),
His mother taught psychiatry, honest I just could have socked her!
She taught her son to exert his mind on animal and friend,
What he did to his pussycat was just about the end.
He purred like other pussycats and always drank his milk
Then that dreadful Stanley put him on the couch
And psychoanalyzed poor pussycat and made him such a grouch.
That pussy's personality slowly began to change
He hissed and arched his back so much he looked like a camel with mange.
He'd sneak into the living room with steps as soft as satin
Climb upon the cocktail bar and mix a strong Manhattan
Throw back his head and gulp it down and lost all sense of reason,
Leering at female pussycats in and out of season.
He'd drink 'til dawn, then down the street he'd stagger round and fat
Soon everyone was gossiping about Stanley's pussycat.
His drinking went from bad to worse, 'twas really most disturbin',
He'd catch the mice at any saloon in trade for a shot of bourbon.
Stanley's pussycat became a drunk; he stole to purchase liquor,

When nice pussycats drink milk and cream Stanley would hiccup and snicker.
Soon he couldn't catch the mice at all; the saloons no longer would pay him,
The mice ran away when he sneaked up on them 'cause his breath would always betray him.
His bloodshot eyes would spot a mouse, he'd lurch in hot pursuit,
And run into the fireplace singing "Mammy" all covered with soot.
He'd see two mice instead of one, sneer, "got you you little mother,"
But the one he grabbed was never for real, he was always catching the other.
Then doom did come as it comes to all, he finally went to the clinic.
The doctor sneered as he examined him, the doctor was a terrible cynic.
His heart beat so awfully fast and even more his pulse, sir,
Stanley's pussycat was switched to cream, he had a pussycat ulcer.

Kovacs read *Mad* while the boys in the *Mad* office, Wallace Wood, Kelly Freas, Wil Elder, and Jack Davis, watched the morning show for ideas. When *Mad for Keeps,* a hard-cover anthology published by Crown Books appeared in 1958, they asked Kovacs to lend his talents to author an introduction. In typical Kovacsian fashion, he fulminated against *Mad*'s habits of expropriating his material and his creations:

Added to my personal feelings about the Mad *staff is my humiliation at witnessing their blatant piracy of my material, surreptitiously changing a comma here and there to disguise the theft. I have watched with* una furtiva lacrima *coursing its melancholy way down my cheek, the abject desecration of my creation, the eminent Cowznofski (corrupted from Cowznowski). I have seen this hallowed Pole's name captioned beneath that ridiculously freckled face of the publisher's mother-in-law. [Ed. note: Alfred E. Newman, formerly Melvin Cowznofski]*

He went on to fervently pray that one day the staff would go broke, and they would have to lend their talents to his own superior enterprises like *The All-Girls' Orchestra Digest, The Zoo Keeper's Monthly,* or *The Two-Headed Calf Owner's Manual.*

Being published in a more dignified though equally freewheeling fashion did come in time. In 1957, Ernie was recognized in certain circles as a brilliant comedian, a brilliant comedic writer, but not as a writer per se. Back in Trenton he was more realistic and wrote for his kolim ridders, "We like to think of ourselves as the bottom rung of literature," but he never approached any publisher with his ideas. As fate would have it, Ken McCormick, an editor at Doubleday and Company, was an avid fan of the *Tonight Show.* A sensible gentleman, otherwise, he was entranced with Ernie's use of television sight-comedy and especially fond of the cheapo epics. Ken wrote a fan letter, then followed it up with a phone call, and learned that Kovacs was dying to get involved with a book — something beyond the visual medium. McCormick found out that Ernie wanted to write a spoof on television. "He knew if he got high-minded and shot it down, no one would want to read it, but if he could catch the level at which he was making people laugh about the very things they were seeing and taking seriously, he would have an audience."

Zoomar, which opened with an ant crossing a brassière into a jar of cold cream and ending with the protagonist, Tom Moore, a rising young television producer, and his wife Eileen, looking toward the western skies of Los Angeles with visions of Big Money in their eyes, was

Ernie's first novel. With McCormick's connivance, Kovacs wrote a few sample chapters on spec and upon approval hacked out the rest in between his other duties. In October, 1957, *Zoomar* hit the streets and smashed its way through to three Doubleday printings and four more Bantam paperback printings. It was a very funny, though critical, book on television, a Candide-like tale of a literary Kovacs (Tom Moore) and his wife Edie (Eileen) awash in the media sea, a story spiced with Fifties tales of payola, tax accountants, slick-talking agents, expense account lunches, dumb sponsors, and insensitive network executives — all spliced together with some conjugal and mercy sex.

Ernie's friends, who appeared in the book with thin disguises, complained. None of them liked it, even if he told the truth as he experienced it:

Any good author must write about what he's aware of, you can't fool around. So what did Ernie do? He had no right exposing his personal life like that — it wasn't flattery. He had no reason to write the book except out of a desire to get published. He did it as an exercise, there was no reason for it, no redeeming values to it . . . I was fourth lead!

Marty Cummer (transposed to Kummel), the agent

I didn't like Zoomar. *I'm one of the few people who knew that the book was written in ten days top to bottom, and all he did was shoot his mouth off. He was capable of a hell of a lot more than that book. He knocked it off for a quick buck between card games.*

Barry Shear

That book he wrote was almost infantile . . . It was early smoking room stuff, early Terry Southern.

Marc Connelly, playwright (not mentioned in *Zoomar*)

McCormick saw through the personalities. "He wrote three or four sample chapters, and they were wonderful and racy and their infectious quality lay in the fact that they weren't carefully honed or written in a polished style. Part of what was delightful was the spontaneity, and underneath it all was a good kick in the pants which got more severe all the time."

Tom Moore starts off with his ideals intact and a job working for an advertising agency. Through a series of misfortunes, he loses his job and becomes a consultant for the Miss Wipe-Ola Beauty Hunt (Wipe-Ola being the name of a shoe polish.) The search for Miss Wipe-Ola is really a blind for an investigation of the corrupt practices of many quiz-type shows well known within the industry, but little examined outside of it. (The scandals attached to programs like *21* and *The $64,000 Question* would make headlines.) Ernie's hero, Moore, somehow survives amorous beauty contestants, scurrilous, though good-natured sponsors, and a tempting job offer for an Omnibus-type show. After many months of back-breaking work, his sponsor cancels because they haven't gotten a handle on the audience.

In the second-to-last chapter, Moore lashes out against the traditional view that the television audiences were composed of 12-year-olds. Kovacs felt that television was an intelligent medium for the entertainment of intelligent men and women, though that theory clashed with the perennial network doublethink: programs cost money, sponsors have money, sponsors are sponsors (i.e., they have the 12-year-old minds), therefore programming must appeal to the sponsors before the public. Television time is too expensive to waste on something which is not a sure commercial success like *Let's Make a Deal* or *Truth or Consequences.*

He told the head of CBS:

We have told the public that this is what you are going to see on this medium — this medium of television, with millions of dollars creating excitement in electronic achievement, a device which is so miraculous in its function that it is thousands of years ahead of its time. An inanimate metal box with a glass lens in front that can show a man shooting a quail two thousand miles away! This metal box has other purposes besides showing cowboys as they looked twenty years ago shooting blanks at each other from behind trees which is becoming as familiar to the television viewer as his next-door neighbor. What shall we do, kill Wide, Wide Worlds, *the* Omnibuses, *the* Meet the Presses *and have an eighteen-hour day of Jimmie Dennis running up and down the aisles, kissing old ladies, and passing out orchids to the funniest hats? When Jimmie poops out, we can fill the waiting time with some Farmer Brown cartoons and English movies. We can even arrange it so that scripts won't have to be written. We can drop a coin in the slot or pull a lever and have a script fall out that the surveys tell us the "morons," who are our surgeons, judges, and priests, should like. We can bring on the newscasts with magic-lantern slides and cartooned drawings of milk strikes so the twelve-year-old idiots who pilot planes, pull teeth, and build houses can understand. What are we going to be? Little Orphan Annies wearing the same red dress for thirty-six years? We can have a Ding Dong night school for adults to prepare them for their day's work ahead. After the nuclear fissionists finish a long day at the lab they can watch two housewives break balloons with spatulas to win a refrigerator.*

If *Zoomar* was "an exercise with no redeeming values" as Marty Cummer, the agent's agent, seemed to think, then it was one hell of an exercise, and a courageous statement to make considering *everyone* knew who Tom Moore really was.

Zoomar was written about the same time Ernie was bidding adieu to New York television, after the January 19, 1957, *Silent Show*. After this success he now had the leverage to deal with NBC. They wanted him to sign another contract. "Maybe I'm being Hungarian with them, but they owe me some money on the balance of my *Tonight* contract, and I'll be damned if I'll talk about my new show until they pay me for the last," said Ernie at the time. "They keep saying, 'Let's get the new show going, then we'll iron out the old show,' but I refuse to let them dangle a small morsel before me which they already owe me."

Success was its own punishment for Ernie Kovacs. He'd done well with shoestring budgets despite the pressure of crushing personal and financial obligations. But now his public and private consumption patterns could overlap. He'd spectacularly blown *The Silent Show's* $35,000 budget all to hell. "Of course it's over," he said flippantly. "Can't let the networks feel secure." Security had nothing to do with it, for Ernie's problem was that the differences between the below-the-line costs (sets, cameras, trucking, special effects, etc.) and the above-the-line costs (producer, guests, talent, writers, etc.) mystified him completely. Hating the cost-accountant network mentality and being a perfectionist even when he couldn't afford it, Ernie made it a point of honor to ruin the budgets of his shows. And now that he'd made the big time, he'd have more opportunities to exercise his ultimately ruinous proclivities.

By mid-1957, Kovacs went to Hollywood: Columbia Pictures was hot for the "Ol' Olive." He thought he'd found a real home where he'd be among his creative equals and where he could create his visions without

Ernie conducting the Simian Orchestra.

restraints, living the life of ease. As he packed up his house and moved, while Edie was working in "Li'l Abner" on Broadway, he mused about his future in the movies. The Borscht Belt refugees from other small towns who'd come to Hollywood before him waited in the wings for the Boy Wonder.

Neither he nor they could know that he only had five more years in which to burn before that fateful phone pole on Santa Monica Boulevard.

If you've been around show business as long as I have . . . there's a truism that sets in with most people, and I don't say you or I would be any different. I say to you, you're making ten thousand a week, and you are . . . you see a Rolls Royce that cost twenty thousand bucks. You start to think, jeez that's only two weeks' pay, OK . . . it's a car, it'll last a few years. It's gotta be less to you mentally than the guy who makes two hundred a week and buys a Ford 'cause he isn't doing it with two weeks' salary. The truth is though, when you get done with the government, you aren't making ten thousand dollars a week by a long shot . . . that's where they get in trouble. I've seen it happen to a lot of guys. Ernie was more flamboyant in his lifestyle. The guys who are less flamboyant would go out and buy a painting for ten thousand dollars that not too many peo-

ple would know they paid ten thousand dollars for. It's the same thing, all of a sudden they're tapped out, and I see it over and over again with clients I have that make good salaries. The business managers are calling me up saying, "Christ, can't you get an advance on the next check?" Ain't got five cents in the bank. As I say Ernie made a thing of being flamboyant.

— Marvin Moss, Ernie's Hollywood agent for MCA

If you're poor, you're considered mediocre; if you're mediocre, you're considered good; if you're good, you're considered a genius; if you're a genius, you don't work. It's such a bullshit town.

— Barry Shear

He had only been in Hollywood once before, and for some reason which he had never been able to determine, he felt he should be on guard. Not seriously on guard, just on guard.

— *Zoomar,* Chapter 45

Hollywood, Herr Hollywood, where all good dreams go, where small town boys with talent go, the dramatics teacher's pet.

Hollywood, where there is nothing to do except play cards and schmooze between takes, or decorously hang out in the best of places; where "style" is the ultimate and there you are with all those other names ...

Hi, aren't you —

I'm Ernie Kovacs, Broadway Bow and Man-About-Town.

Not Hollywood, no, Hollywood is funky, down near Western Avenue off the Boulevard, or back in the hills near Griffith Park, or above the Sunset Strip — grit city sometimes — no, not Hollywood. Beverly Hills is *the* Hollywood, where the garage attendants in the 9000 Building know more about cars than the patrons who drive. Dual Ghias or Mercedes 230s, where money is the key and taste of no consideration. The ugliest suburb subcity in the world outside of Levittown with $350,000 houses built on acre plots. Miles and miles of blank sidewalks, where walking is a capital offense. Even the hitchhikers on Sunset Strip in Beverly Hills check out the cars that stop; even they can't afford to be seen in a cheap car, no sir.

Beverly Hills spreads its neon thighs to square miles of bad taste liberally sprinkled with Mexican chintz; home of the Hollywood syndrome, put simply by Shear, as always never flinching, " . . . you can invite anybody to a party in Hollywood and they'll show up — I don't care who the hell it is, Kirk Douglas, Gary Cooper . . . send them a letter, they'll come to your house. "There's nothing going on in this town anyway — that is if you're in." Kovacs was in. They came in droves.

They specialize in privacy, these heavies who've been delegated to play out celluloid fantasies for the money. They discover in time chintzy joints with bad food to be seen in — PJ's, Nicky Blair's, or Dominic's where the maître d' knows everyone there is to know and you can't get in unless you are who you are. The menu is simple, you can memorize the specials in a few sessions. Quiet places where there are no press agents, celebrity fucker/gawkers, where they can come in off the set with greasepaint still on their faces for a steak and Scotch in Hollywood, Herr Hollywood.

Hollywood runs on warm bodies, warm flesh, $100 hookers' commutation specials from the Sands or Tahoe, to be rented from the Polo Lounge. Undiscovered flesh lines the pool, tits hanging, awaiting a mogul to plunk them on casting-audition couches, to take them off to stardom. It is the home of the big time spenders, drinkers, and the tax collector.

The Hollywood Ernie Kovacs knew was filled with big-time spenders and body inhabitors, looking for the newest kick, the in-est in, another winner to call their own. They were captivated by what they'd seen while being loyal to Lewis. Kovacs, who had never been part of anywhere, really a visitor, bemused spectator of the human zoo and personality, became Hollywood property along with the other tinsel dreams who'd preceded him. Hollywood for the Olive was like candyland complete with the stars, the steam baths, and the all-night card games with Sinatra, Deano, Lemmon, parties with Edward G. Robinson, and Jimmy Stewart. When you're hot in Hollywood, everyone wants to be your friend, having nothing to do with talent at all. Talent is something unrelated to box office.

Better die when you're hot in Hollywood — no room for losers here.

When you come to Hollywood, the Business opens its arms to you: welcome to the outpost, Ern, welcome to the club. When you're famous and hot and die in Hollywood, your friends come to mourn and preserve your memory like spun-gold tapestry. When you die in Hollywood, the agents represent you to the graveside while screening your friends at the service. When you die in Hollywood and a writer comes to seek you out, those "friends" hide behind the lure of Hollywood and the mystique they've so painfully erected to keep everyone out, especially the uninitiated. You've got to be initiated, Ern, before they choose to tell you, for your friends assume to be the keepers of your soul and the maintainers of your myth and theirs. "He's my best friend," they all say.

In Hollywood, the "talent never mingles with the technicians unless on set, while the technicians stay to themselves and bemusedly watch the agents who run like harried rats between the producers, directors, "stars," and the government in a dance of exquisite death and $100 lunches. Having a good agent in Hollywood is imperative, if you esteem to be a hot property. The agent is your flack, your confidant, your gin partner, and your mother. He gives you to other agents who specialize in your personality more — and you become initiated, and they become maintainers of your myth and theirs. "He's my best friend," they all say. Everyone — and no one — was Ernie's best friend.

Only one Ernie Kovacs and only one myth; the reality of the poker table, late-night gin sessions, and the steam room, drinking wine in the wine cellar with the plastic cobwebs on the racks, king of the grown-up little boys' room. You become as real as the turntables on your driveway or that cigar; you become your own caricature. And yet those shades persist. Searching for friends in the biz is like searching for that pot of gold with the tax assessor over your shoulder, and the business goes on inexorably and your style remains for all that is Hollywood, Herr Hollywood.

Candyland to you, where all those dreams coalesced into a spontaneous vision of creative freedom. Being a success in Hollywood and maintaining your own personality is hard work. Ingratiating yourself, being your own walking image, being yourself in spite of the Hollywood syndrome — or because of it.

Adulation is transitory in Hollywood, in the all-consuming search for winners. Breaking the mold to be yourself is nearly impossible among the big spenders and box-office winners. And how do you proceed to be yourself when you inalterably are?

Holy shit, here I am with Edward G. Robinson and Kim Novak (she's a sweet girl) and Shirley MacLaine (a kook but great) and Marilyn Monroe . . . gee. Hollywood, Herr Hollywood in the late Fifties when you were burning strong, having fun, and spending money. Just like Moss said, " . . . the money was there and you said, 'Hey let's go to dinner tonight,' and there's no fucking reason why you had to go to dinner, but you went to dinner, and you went to a fancy restaurant and you spent a hundred and fifty bucks for the three of you — nobody gave a shit. You wrote it off on the business."

The agents have seen it all, Ern. Resurrected so many times, Lazarus is old schtick to them. Once you move to Hollywood, you become part of the myth. They won't let you escape now, a fly caught in amber in a $100,000 den always on display, always a contender.

But who would ever believe that Hollywood is just like Trenton, New Jersey. . .but it is, Ern, it was, and where is freedom then?

• • •

When Ernie Kovacs first came to Hollywood and was living at the Beverly Hills Hotel while shooting *Operation Madball,* he was approached by Henry Rogers, of the public relations firm of Rogers, Cowen, and Brenner, who tried to woo him into the firm. "Look, we'll even get you a *Life* magazine cover if ya sign with us, Ern." While Henry was barraging the Olive with hot type, Ernie was slowly backing up to the front desk. When Rogers finally allowed some breathing space, Kovacs asked for his morning mail.

"Certainly, Mister Kovacs, coming right up," said the clerk.

Ostentatiously placed on top of the incoming mail was a pre-release copy of the latest issue of *Life* magazine; Ernie's face was already on the front cover.

At the beginning, Ernie treated it all like part of that cheapo epic he'd already written countless times before. Candyland . . . and Ernie had a sweet tooth. Hollywood had a sweet tooth for Kovacs, the guy who blew Lewis off the Trendex on January 19, 1957, with the sound of no hands clapping. He'd been playing the same reels over and over in his mind for ages and there he finally was. The bright lights of Broadway paled against the lush, moldy elegance of Tinseltown. Surely, he reasoned, this community would recognize his peculiar talents as a creative artist and give him the elbow room he demanded. He was close to achieving that dream. Television had served its purpose, he thought, and since Columbia Pictures had signed him, he thought he could be the matinee idol that he was with Contemporary Players. Not quite.

The Hollywood movie community did accept him with open arms, for they too were mesmerized. They wanted Kovacs the comedian, the comedic actor, not Kovacs the student of drama. They had no place for bright-eyed boy wonders from an untested medium, even 37-year-old aging boy geniuses. Hollywood at that time was still looking for handsome replicas of the old guard — the public demanded it. Besides, according to Edd Henry, who represented Ernie in the movies for MCA, "There was no popular Hollywood actor who had a big black mustache, and Kovacs was too specialized a talent to carry any picture himself. A Tyrone Power he wasn't."

Instead of making Ernie the center of attention, which he obviously couldn't be, Henry found him parts in which he could show off his talents safely while more handsome actors played the leads. In short, Ernie was typecast with a vengeance, and since he had no script approval with his large-figure Columbia contract, he made do as comedic villain, a captain in the anonymous armed forces, or a plain funny thief. In four of his nine movies Ernie was *The Captain*: Capt. Paul Locke, a regulation-eatin', fire-breathin', walking wet blanket in *Operation Madball* (1958); a genially corrupt Cuban chief of Police, Capt. Ségurra in *Our Man In Havana* (1960); another indeterminate (as was the picture) Captain Stark in *Wake Me When It's Over* (1960); an outrageously tippling bumbler, The Captain, in *Sail A Crooked Ship* (1962).

Ernie as Henry Foster Malone, the "World's Meanest Man" in *That Jane From Maine*.

The Captain strikes again, this time, in *Operation Mad Ball*.

In between captain roles, Ernie played two writers: Sidney Redlich in *Bell, Book and Candle* (1959), who specialized in the occult and had a rabid taste for gin, and Roger Altar, an eccentric in *Strangers When We Meet* (1960). Even a few plain nasty SOBs were good roles for Kovacs like Frankie Cannon in *North to Alaska,* and Henry Foster Malone in *It Happened to Jane* (1959), which was a "sleeper" and was released by the studio three times with three different titles: *That Jane From Maine, The Wreck of the Old '97,* and *Mrs. Casey Jones,* all of which did little for the film's commercial success.

Unfortunately, the only film which Ernie did in Hollywood with substance to it (besides an unreleased short in 1958 called *Showdown at Ulcer Gulch* starring Edie Adams, Bing Crosby, Chico and Groucho Marx, Bob Hope, Salome Jens, and Orson Bean) was an obscure film directed and produced by Mario Zampi called *Five Golden Hours.* Co-starring Cyd Charisse and George Sanders, Ernie played Aldo Bondi, petty crook and professional mourner, who specialized in swindling wealthy widows out of their ermine socks. Bondi, however, meets up with his female counterpart Sandra (Cyd Charisse), a sleek Italian Vampirella-type who has buried more husbands than she can remember. Together they plan a caper involving the time differential between New York and Rome, but in the shuffle Sandra escapes with the loot. Bondi disappears into a madhouse to escape the law, and meets George Sanders, another thief feigning madness. They break out and go after another wealthy widow.

In the last reel, Sandra re-appears and Bondi foolishly marries her, after which, his fortune and his suave debonair manner push up daisies while Sandra counts the loot. *Five Golden Hours* was only a step above many of the wholesome family-type pictures which Kovacs appeared in with the likes of Doris Day or Jack Lemmon. The closest he ever came to a dramatic part was in a movie about adultery, *Strangers When We Meet,* a woefully ponderous turkey of a film where he played the eccentric Roger Altar, a writer, at whose half-built house the amours of Kirk Douglas and Kim Novak occur.

Ernie's celluloid career was not the stellar success that he had wished for, though the agents in charge, Henry and Moss, did their best given their highly individualistic client and the prevailing attitudes at the studio.

It was my feeling with Ernie that he was a personality, rather than a romantic image, and if you wanted to hold a picture you had to have a romantic image. If the picture was a failure, you were a failure. Now if you were an important star of the day, if you were Ty Power and you had six or seven hits behind you, you could afford two or three failures. But he [Ernie] didn't have that position so he didn't have a right to go ahead and go to the forefront and lead with his chin when he was really a personality and a fine actor. He belonged in that type of characterization and he could live a long, long time. He always ended up being equally billed (we always fought for billing) and we always had the roles that entitled him to that position. In many of the films that didn't work, he always got basically good reviews.

— Edd Henry

You know he did some pictures in which he was great in what he did, and the reviewers came out and said, "Jesus, Ernie Kovacs was great in those two scenes, but he should have had more to do." That picture that Quine directed [Strangers When We Meet] *was not a turkey because of Ernie Kovacs; the general reaction to Ernie in the picture was good.* It Happened to Jane *went out with three different titles, but the reviews never panned Kovacs. Some of the pictures were bum pictures, but no one ever blamed Ernie. Ernie wasn't supposed to be carrying the picture*

Ernie as Aldo Bondi in *Five Golden Hours*. (This page and following page)

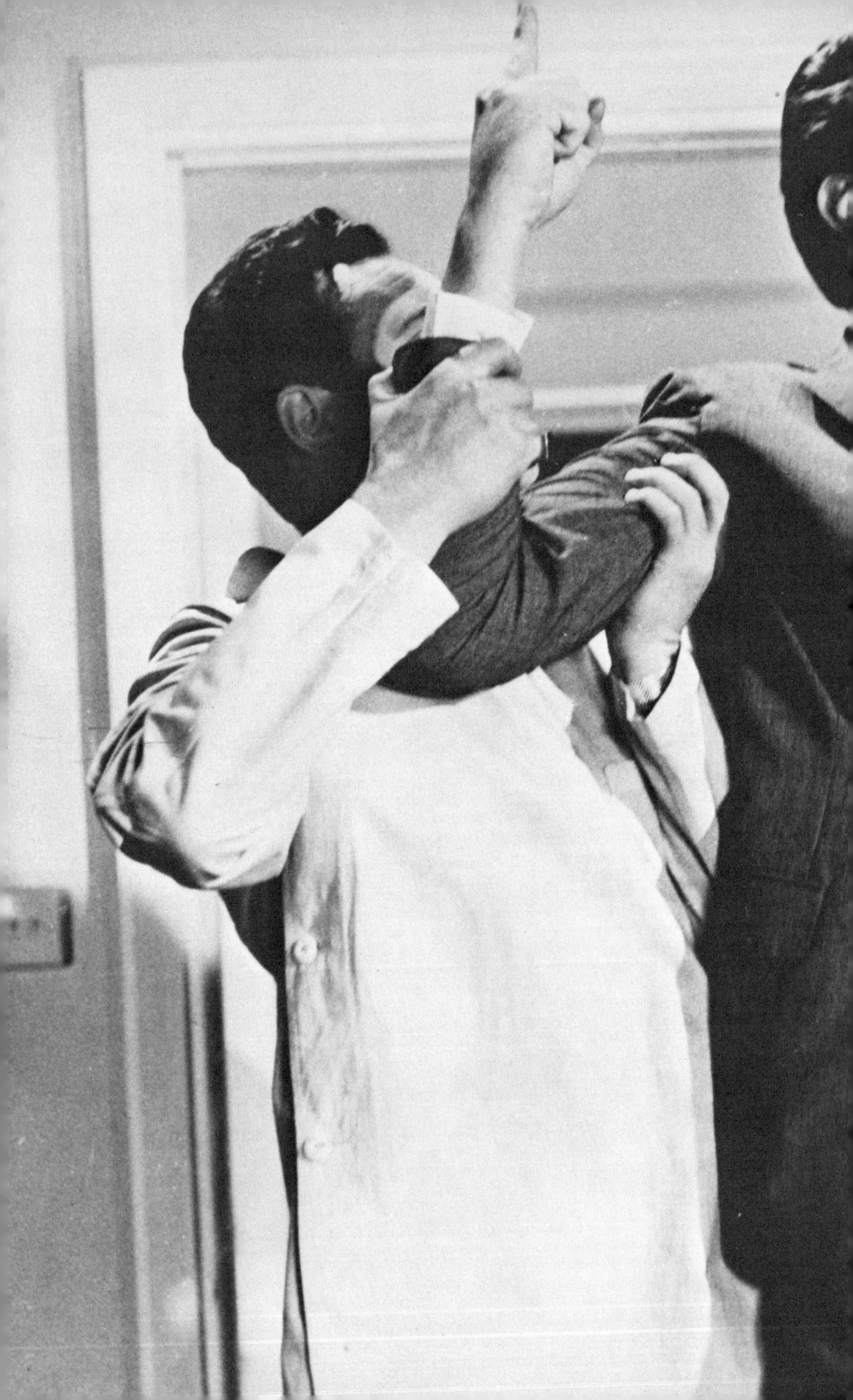

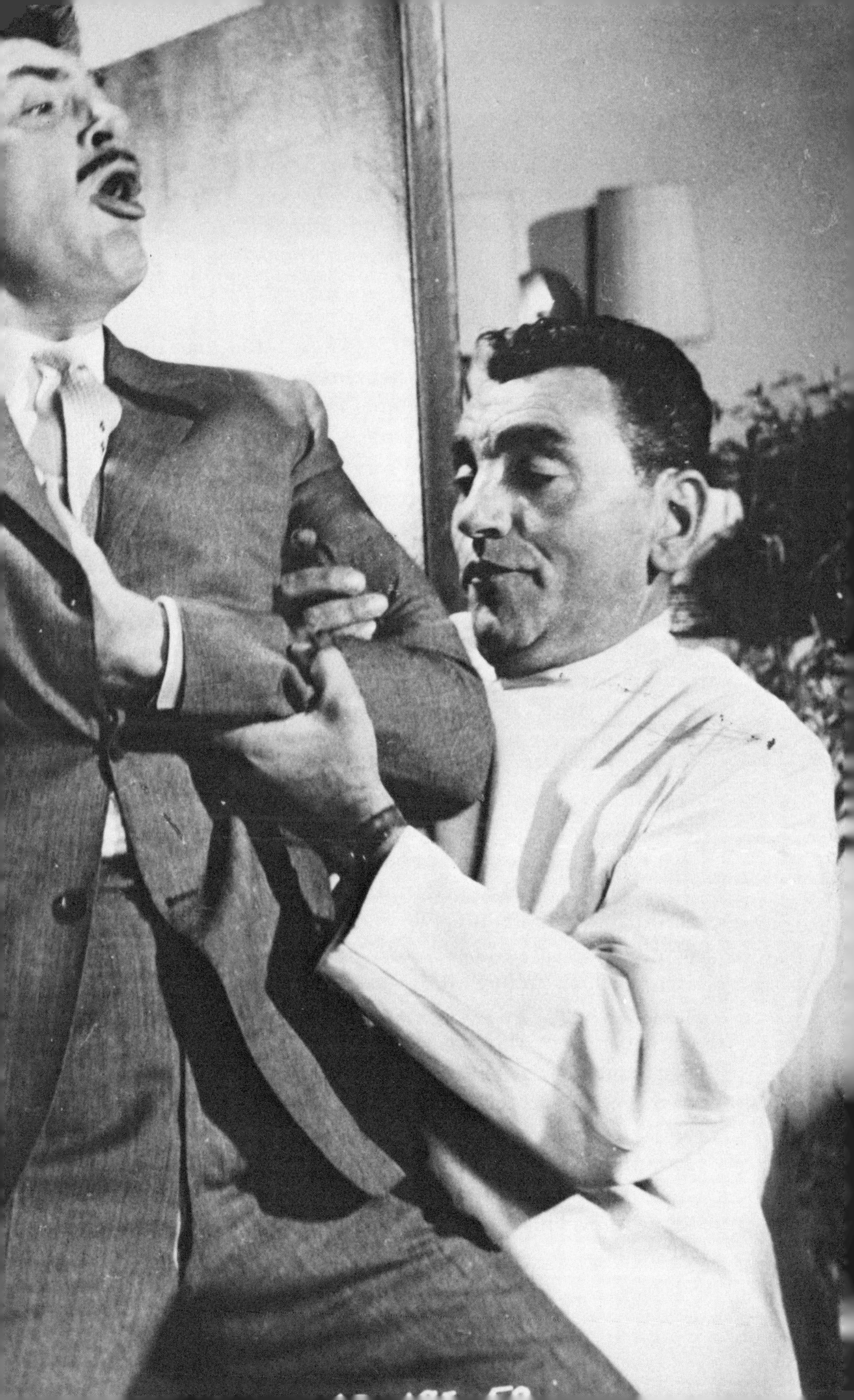

and I give great credit to Edd Henry, who planned his career that way, 'cause Edd Henry, who knew better, said, "He isn't a star, but I'll protect him, and he'll keep getting those kind of parts and no one will know."

— Marvin Moss

Ernie knew, or at least felt he knew better than they. "No more #* #!! captains" was his *Variety* retort. He'd have to wait until his Columbia contract ran out, then he'd shop around for a better deal — if it could be had.

Television was not entirely forgotten in the first rush of Hollywood. In his incessant need to perform, he became a professional host/guest for many varieties of NBC weekend entertainment specials in lieu of his own show. He capered, he danced, he mugged, and he pantomimed with George Gobel, Dinah Shore, Polly Bergen, and even Perry Como for whom he demonstrated his famous disappearing-girl trick with the ultimate discrete girl-friend (Barbara Loden) dressed from head-to-toe in black velour covered with a white winding sheet. Unwind the sheet using another camera, superimpose, and presto — no more explanations to the F.W.

Not that he didn't *mind* being a professional guest, but that wasn't the reason he'd gone into television in the first place. He really liked performing. When hosting an NBC Saturday Night producers' special called *Festival of Magic* he subtly hinted his displeasure. Masquerading as Motzah Hepplewhite, an inept illusionist, Ernie persuaded what appeared to be a network executive to step into a specially constructed box through which he ran swords, astounding home viewers with this world-famous illusion. The trick worked well enough. The swords went in carefully until they struck something rigid . . . Scratch one executive.

Two years and a few months after the silent show, Kovacs again had his own special, *Kovacs on Music,* for which he imported most of his NBC morning production staff headed by Shear the outspoken. It premiered on May 22, 1959, and was a compendium of his old material perfected and augmented with a $ whopping budget.

This el cheapo production opened with a shot of a long-handled ax deeply imbedded in a typewriter surrounded by a few crumpled pieces of paper and an empty booze bottle over which was superimposed the words: "Written and Produced by Ernie Kovacs." Ernie welcomed the viewers from the control room, cigar smoldering in his hand, with, "I have never really understood classical music so I would like to take this hour to explain it to others. There most certainly should be a definite place in television for this type of program, as I have a crying need for money." As he turned around to watch the monitors in front of him, the show officially opened with a solitary broken-down rendition of Ernie's tune, *The Oriental Blues,* but after a few bars in a flash of Hollywood elegance, the curtains swung open to reveal André Previn and a 70-piece orchestra dressed in tails, finishing off the tune with flashy orchestration. For the following hour Ernie did indeed explain music in all forms and guises. He even threw in "Swan Lake," but no rendition anyone had ever heard before. Ernie used ballerinas dressed in gorilla suits for the finale!

Definitely not the run-of-the-mill NBC spectacular, the finale was the end of all ends. "This is the finale and will have everyone in it, but Moisha Pipek," said Ernie in the script's final draft. "The full choral group will be used in this [and will] all be dressed in Valkyrie costumes with one in a basketball uniform with knee pads, holding a ball." The finale parodied everybody from Wagner to Jeanette MacDonald and Nelson Eddy. Edie the Valkyrie meeting Ernie the Mountie all scrupulously scripted and ad libbed. Play now in Kovacsland between the clutching ferns, falling sets, and missed cues!

Kovacs on Music also contained a very old bit which Ernie had first done back in Philadelphia, where he had electronically matted himself into an old Boris Karloff film. In his version of *Blue Tail Fly* Ernie mixed animated cartoon figures and live images, throwing in a cartooned blue tail fly in top hat and tails, carrying a cane, assisted by two flies (on scale no doubt). The whole idea, which took five minutes of air time, was fiendishly arranged and executed.

• • •

Despite the attendant raves of the critics, NBC wasn't going to buy another series of Kovacs' visions. He still needed visibility as a public figure and when things seemed bleak, fate stepped in bearing all manner of strange gifts, including cigars.

Around the time of *Kovacs on Music,* freelance producers Peter Arnel and Irving Manesfield (husband of Jacqueline Suzanne, a former guest on Ernie's Dumont morning show) along with the Consolidated Cigar Company, makers of Dutch Masters cigars, were shopping around for a host for a quiz show they'd just sold to ABC TV. Not much of a vehicle really — dumb in fact. After a series of skits about historical events, the panelists were supposed to guess *which* event — yuk, yuk. Actually Dutch Masters was more interested in finding someone to sell their cigars, like Groucho Marx was doing with *You Bet Your Life.* When George Burns, another famous TV cigar smoker, turned them down, they naturally thought of Kovacs to whom cigars were as much a part of life as breathing.

Arnel and Manesfield approached Marvin Moss, Ernie's television agent, and gave him a print of the pilot. Ernie was not impressed, after all he'd made up far better shows with no sponsors. Marvin had Ernie half-talked into it on

July 4 when he brought Buddy Silverman, the president of Consolidated Cigar, and another older gentleman, a real cigar maker, up to Ernie's house. They chatted, they pitched, but if Ernie didn't approve the sponsor, there would be no show. The moment of truth approached when Ernie finished one of his own Havanas. About five minutes went by in silence, Ernie started to reach for another when the old tobacco guy said, "How would you like a Dutch Masters cigar?"

The agent couldn't breathe, knowing Ernie and his outspoken views. Conceivably the whole deal was riding on dead vegetable matter.

A deathly hush settled over the den while Ernie lit up and took a drag.

"You know," he said, exhaling, "when I was getting over TB, my father came to see me and handed me a cigar, the kind he always smoked — a Dutch Master. You know, it's not a bad cigar."

The agent was relieved, "Well, the whole fucking room lit up and I figured the deal was made, and it was. He wasn't bullshitting them."

Free cigars? Shades of State Street and Mister Moscowitz.

The packagers hired Kovacs all right, but if they expected to exercise any control over what he did on *Take a Good Look,* they were mistaken, especially if they thought he'd stick to their rules. "Come on, what are we kidding ourselves?" he told them. "We're only on because I'm smoking cigars for Dutch Masters, and you can take the rules and stick them up your ass; there are no such things as rules. We're going to do a show and have fun, and who cares whether it's right or wrong." He further informed Milt Hoffman, and outside producers Arnel and Manesfield were called in to "oversee" Ernie's budget. "I can do this comedy the way I want without anyone saying, 'Hey it isn't funny,' because it doesn't have to be funny.

It's a clue and no one can criticize me." So he had it covered both ways.

TAGL turned out to be a cross between a weekly Kovacs special and a continuing parody of a quiz show. With the help of a new gang of actors who included Jolene Brand, Bobby Lauher, Joe Miklos (a card-playing friend), and an aspiring model, Maggie Brown, Kovacs did perform skits with clues as per format, but no one could figure out what they were, as in the case of this fairly typical script for the clue indicating the phrase "Beat the German by a Broad Jump."

This is a little area, two banks which should be about five feet apart, not too steep so that Kovacs can jump from one bank to the other. There is water, some bushes, etc. Kovacs is Huckleberry Finn-type of boy. Tie a handkerchief around his toe like they do for bandages in Huck Finn-type things. He is fishing with a bamboo pole and a string, suddenly he feels a bite and he starts pulling. We show the entire scene and we see that he is pulling something sticking out of the water. We take a close up of it and see that is is a periscope sticking out of the water. We take a close-up of a U-boat commander. . .There is a very simple set so don't everybody get alarmed. It only has to be about four feet wide and look like the interior of a sub. It can be an iron-looking flat with rivets on it, and a periscope hanging, and Bobby [Lauher] is looking into the periscope. Bobby does a German accent: Himmel! Achtung mit der torpedo tubes. Fire von! (cut back to Kovacs) *Now we see the wake of the torpedo toward Kovacs. Now this thing may sound frantic, fantastic and costly, but all we need is some underwater thing shooting out some carbon gas from that periscope toward the bank where Kovacs is sitting. We'll show this is the water. Kovacs sees it. Gives a broad jump and jumps to the other side of the bank. The torpedo hits, and we want a big flash pot to go up with a big explosion, and cut fast to black: no dissolve.*

Broad jump — get it?

The panelists, Hans Conreid, Caesar Romero, and Edie Adams, rarely if ever guessed the clues or the answer.

TAGL was quite a commercial success for Dutch Masters, but Trendex-wise it was a flop. The 12-million-plus viewers which *The Untouchables* delivered at 10:30 Thursday nights dropped to 4 million in a short time after the show's inception. ABC affiliates cancelled in droves and just about everybody was screaming about this cockamamie show, except the sponsors who were selling cigars like crazy. Ernie was relatively happy because he'd met a sponsor who didn't try to control his pitch. Furthermore, the sponsor encouraged him to develop his own silent commercials which became classics in themselves. With a Hayden String Quartet for background music, Kovacs produced a variety of unusual commercial visions. Passing through a museum, Ernie genially offers a statue of Napoleon a cigar and is refused. On second try, Napoleon relents, but when he takes his hand out of his vest to accept the gift, his pants fall down. In another commercial Ernie appeared as a firing squad victim whose final request is to smoke a cigar. The aroma is so beguiling that the members of the squad drop their rifles and crowd around to inhale the heavenly fragrance, much to the consternation of *El Capitán*. Viewers even watched Ernie steaming in a cannibal stewpot. After the chief has lighted the fire, Ernie silently remonstrates until he returns to light Ernie's unlit cigar. He happily puffs away as the camera pans down to a box of Dutch Masters beside the smoldering cauldron. Thanks to Ernie, Dutch Masters received a wide appreciation, while Ernie himself received a Cleo, advertising's equivalent of an Oscar, for his spots.

Haltingly, *Take a Good Look* managed to run through the fall season of 1959 and into the spring of 1960 before it was cancelled for lack of interest. Jack Mogulescu, Consolidated's vice-president in charge of Ernie, was loathe to turn loose their new symbol, and made him the host of *Silents Please* a summer showcase of vintage films which Ernie introduced from his den. TAGL returned briefly for the fall season but died in the spring of 1961, though Consolidated was still casting around for a cigar vehicle for their favorite salesman. Mogulescu offered Ernie another shot, a series of monthly hour-long specials beginning in the spring of 1961. Whatever he wanted.

Commencing April 20, 1961, and continuing monthly until after his death in January, 1962, the specials were the Olive's most spectacular, expensive, and extensive undertakings in his video career. They served as a compendium of 12 years of television experience. Even though much of the material was already "old hat" to many viewers, it was a challenge to the men and women who worked for him to create what are still considered television's finest comedic hours.

There was very little that was normal about Ernie's production techniques when he was going full tilt, 27 hours straight in marathon taping sessions, predictably running headlong into ABC's own ideas about how television shows ought to be run. An excerpt from a letter that Scott Runge, network production coordinator, wrote to Sandy Cummings, the network head, about Special Number 3 taped May 28, 1961, is fairly typical of the Kovacs pace.

Ernie Kovacs Special Number 3 ran the usual course on May 28, 1961, with men in at midnight, Saturday, May 27, and the final wrap finishing at 6:00 ﬃ.=.*, Monday, May 29. A quick rundown of finishing this show: two men in special effects and three in electric out at 4:30* ﬃ.=.*, four stage-*

hands out at 5:00 ffi.=., and six engineers out at 6:00 ffi.=. Two videotape men out at 6:00 ffi.=. and 7:30 ¹.=. Most of the crew dropped by ones and twos beginning at 7:00 ¹.=. Sunday, May 28.

Fairly typical. And although the brass may have objected to the schedule, the crew loved it all. They loved the challenging work, the Triple Golden overtime pay, the great food and wine that went along with the work.

People would pull rank just to work on the show. The crews were treated like humans, not union cards. "The executives said," according to Bob Kemp, now an ABC technical director who then worked for Ernie as a cameraman as well as the unit's still photographer, " 'We got all these rules, we gotta play by them,' But Ernie wouldn't do that. We would stop for lunch at 11:00 if someone was hungry, or we'd just keep working if we were having a good time, it didn't matter. It cost twenty-five percent more, or whatever it was, if you go past a certain hour. That didn't matter at all. 'We're going to go, we're having a good time, right guys' he'd say. And that was fine, it didn't matter. No other show like it."

There was always premium beer and wine on set for casual thirst, and catering was, of course, an added expense. For his third special, Ernie spent $995 for pizzas, wine, and soda from the Villa Capri; for his seventh special he laid out $675 for a sit-down dinner for 85. No wonder crews jockeyed for the show!

No expense was spared, especially when it came to special effects. ABC possessed Bob Hughes in special effects to whom Ernie always used to say he was indebted. Bobby manufactured many of Ernie's more outrageous stunts and sight gags. For one three-second bit he constructed a 500-gallon tank to be placed behind a map of the Hoover Dam. When some official pointed at the map, the dam was supposed to break, washing out a conference room full of people. "We had it in a forklift," said Hughes. "We made a great big tank and had a chute, which came down and up so that the water just dropped into the chute, and then flew about twenty feet. It was supposed to wipe out all these people sitting around a conference table. Ernie got scared of it when he saw it, and just did it with one guy."

Bobby once spent three days chasing a drop of water around the studio. The skit was supposed to trace the life of a raindrop from the sky, to the stream, into a tap, down a drain, into a sewer, and finally out to sea. The ending was supposed to be when a sea gull drank the raindrop and flew off, "but they had a heck of a time getting that pigeon to fly . . . threw rocks at it, everything. It wouldn't move. We turned him loose and he just sat there."

Hughes was also responsible for the construction of a gigantic cuckoo clock which, when opened while striking the hour, revealed a bird roasting on a spit. Costing $2,500 and used only once, the cuckoo clock still sits somewhere in the ABC effects department. The most expensive creation that Bobby put together for Ernie was a car drop for a blackout in which Ernie, as a used-car salesman demonstrating the durability of his product, was supposed to touch the fender. Instead of the car collapsing, the pavement beneath the car crumbled and the auto dropped from sight. Cost: $12,000. He also built a breakaway plane where, when Ernie cranked up the engine in the cockpit, the stick and motor took off while the main section of the aircraft collapsed.

Obviously, they both enjoyed each other, and Ernie was always giving Bobby new gadgets to develop, either for TAGL or the specials, as challenges. "The toughest thing he ever asked me for was the last thing. 'Bobby, for next season, think about square bubbles.' I thought about them for three months and finally gave up. He finally got to me, he finally asked for something I couldn't give him." He never had a chance to tell him either. For his favored special-effects wizard, Ernie regularly sent cases of Valpolicella Bartolini, and when Bobby was married, he sent the newlyweds a silver chafing dish as a wedding present. It's no wonder his crews worked their asses off for him, since Bobby's treatment was standard for all crew members.

The Specials themselves contained many old characterizations, but almost no Percy Dovetonsils. It seemed everyone loved Percy except a certain ABC executive. It is interesting to note that in all the years Dovetonsils trilled, the only adverse comment Ernie received was from someone who thought Ernie was making fun of nearsighted people. This particular executive once objected to a Dovetonsils sequence where Percy was reading from a book called *Four Letter Words* (must be something filthy about that!). Kovacs was adamant, "Star is a four-letter word, what's wrong with that?"

Despite official disdain for Percy, the crews loved him the most and went so far as to play an expensive practical joke on Ernie using Percy. Bob Haley, a cameraman on the show, beside being a close on-set associate of Ernie, was also a masterful impersonator of Dovetonsils's mannerisms down to the lisp. With the connivance of 20 members of the technical staff two hours before Ernie was supposed to take a Percy bit, Haley dressed as Percy taped a complete phony routine. A few hours later, Kovacs repeated the bit for the show, and after it was completed, Gene Lukowsky the technical director asked Ernie if he wanted to see it again.

"No, I think it will be okay," said Ernie, almost blowing the bit.

Lukowsky insisted, "Ernie I think you'd better look at it because we may have a technical problem." The monitor was wheeled over while another camera secretly taped the outcome. "So he's looking at it and he had a drink 'cause it

Ernie as Fidel Castro.

was Percy Dovetonsils and he really did have a drink there, so he's sipping and watching the monitor and all of a sudden," remembers Lukowsky, "this puzzled look came to him [Kovacs watching Haley doing Kovacs], and, staring, he did a take and said, 'Who the fuck is *that*?' And of course we all broke up." That little joke required the cooperation of many people and cost somebody, probably the unknown Percy hater, a few hundred off-the-account dollars. It was definitely worth it.

The Dovetonsils caper was typical of Ernie's attitude about creative freedom; anybody who stood in the way of his expression was a target for anger. On set, Ernie was for the most part a loveable, patient, exacting craftsman who wasn't afraid to take his time to achieve. "He loved to insult authority," said Milt Hoffman. "He hated executives as a whole . . . people who he thought were bugging him, though he sometimes went overboard when he didn't get what he wanted. Once during a taping he called Ollie Treyz, ABC's president, a 'fag' for no good reason." One of the engineers sent it up the organizational tube to the front office. "Just because you are pissed off about something, you don't do that in a studio warm-up," Hoffman concluded. Somehow Ernie got away with it.

When the Specials commenced, the outspoken Shear had been dropped as Ernie's director because of his frictions with the crews, who threatened to resign if he wasn't fired. Actually Shear left midway through *Take a Good Look* because of the dispute, and his place was filled by Joe Behar, Ernie's former Philadelphia director who'd come west with *Wide, Wide World*. Behar basically followed Ernie's orders, since besides writing and acting, Ernie was also directing most of the show from the floor with the aid of a dollied car, using six monitors strapped together.

In his quest to improve his standing in the community, Ernie joined the Director's Guild, though by the end of

1961 the novelty of directing was wearing off. Behar helped some with the editing, though Ernie still did most of it himself along with Milt Hoffman, who had his own problems working for his energetic boss in such close familiarity. "I'm a nonsmoker, but I used to get home after some of those long sessions and burn my clothes because I couldn't get the cigar smoke out." Along with many others, Milt was flabbergasted by Ernie's energy. Not many people knew he was living on three hours' sleep.

After one of those marathon sessions Ernie wanted Hoffman to help him edit some tape. Hoffman couldn't move. "Ah, let's go edit. I'll tell you what I'll do," said Kovacs, "you think you're in such good shape, I'll race you down from the studio to the tape room." The studio was 250 yards away. "I'll beat you, cigar smoking and all." Kovacs won.

Speaking of endurance, the Specials produced their own classic of technical endurance for the crews, a bit which is still talked about today on the ABC lot in Los Angeles. For one show Ernie conceived of a sketch called "Jealousy," a musical *mise-en-scène* that employed the services of an entirely automated, syncopated office where the file cabinets acted like slide trombones, the switchboard light piccoloed, and the water cooler gurgled on cue. A straight-forward idea in principle, it was an expensive, complex time-consuming tour de force which taxed the production staff to the point of mania. Many of Ernie's sight gags were complex, but for this one Hoffman asked Ernie to enclose explanatory sketches along with a memo just to be on the safe side. The reader can only wryly chuckle with Ernie's prefatory crack, "The following is going to be either the downfall of us technically or at least mentally." He wasn't kidding . . .*

*The Appendix II notes on "Jealousy" give testimony enough to the truth.

Obviously there was an astronomical amount of money spent on editing and taping these gags, but whoever made up the working budgets for the Specials in the front office knew little about television, and even less about Ernie's approach and use of it. The first Special aired April, 1961, for example, was budgeted in the recording phase for $2,500 — 25 hours all told. Ernie nearly doubled the figure by the time he finished taping 42 1/2 hours at a cost of $4,437. The second Special's budget raised the figure to 32 hours, but Ernie still used 44 hours. You'd think the front office would have budgeted 40 hours by the second time through.

With or without the budget director, the Specials were masterpieces of editing. " . . . and in every edit in those half-hour shows, there were as many as fifty edits cut with a razor blade, which takes a lot of time," said Hoffman. "Ernie was doing things that were damned impossible to do with tape in those days." Imagine what it took to make "Jealousy" work after the taping of those separate bits of business. The editing room must have looked like a Christmas tree with an advanced case of "tinselitis."

The marathon work schedules for the crews naturally coincided somehow with the whirlwind pace Ernie was keeping outside of the tape room.

Leaving Dovetonsils devotees and overworked technical directors for a moment, we crossfade and redissolve to Hollywood, 1957, to view another transformation of the Olive to Beverly Hills Boy with plenty of chips, collecting the images of champagne tastes in champagne city.

Whether Kovacs overwhelmed Hollywood or Hollywood overwhelmed the Olive is a moot point. To Hollywood, Kovacs was exotic, freewheeling, loveable, human, and very funny. His attitudes about money and good fellowship offset the stylized attitudes of the so-called "Ratpack," that set of Peck's Bad Boys that included among their membership Frank Sinatra, Dean Martin, Peter Lawford, Sammy Davis, Jr., Jack Lemmon, Shirley MacLaine, and Joey Bishop. Collectively they espoused a locker-room comraderie, neat and clean images of gay and free entertainers always on tap for hijinks and a shot of bourbon. They were ebulliently high on the fast life — fast racing machines, poker, beautiful women, lavish parties — the whole catastrophe.

This was more like what Ernie had in mind for his own Hollywood scenario. He'd done it all in New York, done up the town right down to the 17-room duplex on Central Park West. He had had a chauffeur, famous cronies, a beautiful talented wife, and eventually, his children. However in New York he had neither the trust nor the budgets commensurate with his abilities. In Hollywood, Ernie got it all, even the recognition he so desperately craved. He certainly was a character and Hollywood fell under his influence, adapting readily to his lifestyle.

Upon arrival, Ernie gravitated to the very highest echelon of Hollywood society on the set of his first motion picture *Operation Madball.* His director was Richard Quine; his first lead, Jack Lemmon, who'd idolized him from afar. They were both intimates of Billy Wilder, one of the giants of the scene. Lemmon, as a joke, used to follow Kovacs around the set of *Madball* nailing down Ernie's unlit cigars, chuckling when Ernie picked them up and they shredded. Finally Ernie told Jack to watch his Harvard ass; he wasn't spending two dollars apiece on nails. "Then I didn't nail them down anymore," said Lemmon, "and I tried a couple of them. Jesus, I think they were soaked with dynamite — the roof of my head went off." Lemmon and the Olive grew increasingly tight, and Ernie started to be introduced around town.

Ernie's family eventually moved into a home in Coldwater Canyon above Beverly Hills at 2301 Bowmont

Drive. A standard sort of Hollywood home: 20 rooms in a rambling ranch with an electrified front gate, swimming pool in the back, a four-car garage. Each member of the family had a separate suite. Edie's held her practice rooms and sewing room. A $100,000 home that Ernie eventually turned into a $600,000 playpen comfortable enough for the family. For himself, nothing less than a dream would suffice since he was living in a dream capital. He constructed in stages over the course of his Hollywood life a den the likes of which none of his new friends had ever seen. Soon enough it became another hangout of the Pack. With poker, booze, and a steam bath. Where else was better?

Originally the den was nothing more than a small room separated from the main house next to the garage where Ernie could barely squeeze in his poker table, his files, his desk, and other assorted electronic gadgets. At the time of his death not only had he expanded it almost three times its original length, but he had also added, with the help of friends, a steam room, a waterfall, two fireplaces, and the underground wine cellar with the fake sprayed cobwebs. The den was like a Victorian study, a symphony of dark wood, armor, old guns, books, heavy-tufted leather chairs, thick rugs, and electronic gadgets — unmistakably Ernie's world.

The most magnificent edifice in that room was, of course, Ernie's desk, a combination electronic-control center and sound studio that included two tape decks, an oscilloscope, hi-fi controls, editing equipment, and a typewriter. From the desk Ernie would monitor all the happenings in the main house through an intricate intercom system, control his steam bath and the railroad turntable that sat in the driveway — not such an extravagance when one realizes that there were always many cars at the house with no place to turn around. Irving Manesfield, in a burst of goodwill, donated that to the cause one Christmas along with a copper-lined sauna. This monument was faced in one corner by a three-foot-high, inlaid, Louis XIV-type clock, perhaps a touch too ornate (not Edie's choice at all), but a fitting bauble and a good paperweight to boot.

Divided from the second and oldest level by a set of heavy dark wood planks with swords, points down, used as railing, was the playroom which contained another fireplace, a bar, refrigerator, small stove, a few more book cases, and a beautifully inlaid green felt card table with recessed pockets — Edie's gift. Naturally enough, over in a corner behind the poker table was a full suit of armor left over from the New York collection. Nothing at all like the old days in Philadelphia, no more need for front doors and drafts. To complete the obvious, not only was there a bathroom but off that was Manesfield's sauna in which Ernie would host occasional steam-bath card games and production meetings.

Built on top of that was a smaller loft space where Ernie stored his files, golf clubs, and spare ornaments. The Pack or anybody else who came felt instantaneously at home in this Kovacs vision of the male environment. No one needed encouragement when Ernie told them to feel free. For the Pack it was possibly the ultimate hangout, but for one of Ernie's close friends, Hans Conreid, it seemed to be "a grown-up little boy's room" — a description with which even Ernie, after some reflection, agreed.

Whatever way it seemed, the den definitively embodied the Kovacs ideal of togetherness yet he believed in togetherness only up to a point . . . .

However, what I think is bad about togetherness, is this current business of His *and* Hers *matching shirts, bathing suits, and hockey sticks. Nothing makes me feel quite as foolish as even the coincidental wearing of the same colors in clothing, let alone a purposeful wearing of the identical things. For instance, when my wife and I are both wearing our polka-dot bathing suits (even though she looks better in a bathing suit than I do), I always feel we look like misguided twins who in some sort of confusion got married. Going on with this, beyond wearing purple slacks when I am wearing them, I also do not want my wife smoking cigars, drinking boilermakers, or playing poker all night. These things are* mine *and* mine *alone, and the enjoyable aspects of all three of them is the fact that I am the* only *one in the family participating in any of these rather enjoyable diversions.*

In the male-dominated world which Ernie hosted, Edie stayed discreetly in the background and enjoyed the informality. She complimented her husband perfectly, as Edd Henry succinctly remarked, "Edie always had dignity and she always wanted to be at least the one that was the real hostess when you came to the house. She was very proper, she would dress, she was gracious, she wanted to be sure that you had whatever you needed. Ernie naturally accepted the elegance she brought to his house. 'Relax and enjoy it, I'm here,' he used to say, 'what else do you need?' "

According to Henry, the main ingredient of the Kovacs's household was informal elegance and Edie provided the key. "All his simpleness was rubbing off on her, but she maintained that air of elegance. When you came to the house of the hostess that Ernie took for granted, you took it for granted because it was so naturally elegant."

Elegance or Edie? Or a bit of both. She'd made the best of the situation, having given up a promising career to come West to be the attractive hostess. If anyone was overshadowed in Hollywood it was Edie Adams, now Mrs. Ernie Kovacs, the stepmother. She became an even better mother, taking on the responsibility for his children's education. Not only did she persuade Ernie to join a church, but she enrolled the children in Sunday School. In deference to her, Ernie built Edie a practice room, a music room, and over the garage an elegant sewing room where she worked on all the children's clothes as well as her own. Whenever Ernie went on location he always brought along his family, making it doubly difficult for any sort of career to mature. When Edie did go on the road herself, Ernie was uneasy.

Kippie and Bette thrived in the rich atmosphere of Hollywood and Ernie's success. They idolized their papa. Bette was so much of a fan that she learned all of his routines. Friends said she was a chip off the old korner herself. Ernie spoiled his children in typical fashion: each had her own wing in the house complete with television sets, telephones, hi-fi's, and even their own special slide which led from their windows to the back-yard pool. Animals of all descriptions found their way into the house: turtles, cats, dogs, and Ernie's special friend, a burro, which sometimes kept him company in the den. Occasionally the animal would go on a rampage and eat a few scripts, but that was part of the fun — nothing like a dispassionate editor on-call at all hours. They were a family as far as it was possible to be a family given Ern's work schedule and his daily habits. Edie, not Ernie, always made plans for weekend trips with the girls and planned Sunday, weeks in advance, for Ernie was into Hollywood with a vengeance.

Not only was Hollywood the movie capital of the day, but also one of the high-roller centers of action, Vegas and Tahoe being only short hops. Any game was fine with the Olive just so long as he could lose. Long before Hollywood, gambling was an obsession bordering on mania, but now with his Dom Perignon tastes, he was beginning to learn how ruinous it could be. He may have been able to beat his cronies in New York to death with money, but here they all had money themselves — they could match him, raise him, even lose, and they'd always have more. Funny money, Hollywood money.

No place for a gambling man's illusions. In those "funzie" games in the den where time froze and the Jack Daniels flowed 'til dawn, Ernie was taken more than a few times by "friends" who, when not acting, were professional card players. In Hollywood or Vegas or wherever he chose to try his questionable luck, friends or no friends, a mark is a mark. Ernie was the archetypal mark. He couldn't have asked for a better profession than acting where the most predominant game is on-set gin — almost as good as a cigar tree, or as bad as a government lien on your life. He played it broad because there was nothing more he could do as gambling overtook his art; a lethal prop so much a part of his character.

Actually one of the reasons Arnel and Manesfield hired Milt Hoffman in the first place was to try to stop Kovacs from playing cards on the set when the crews were ready. He was always pleading in his dressing room, "One more hand, one more hand," while the budget was being shot to hell. Cards were so much a part of his routine that when he first met Hoffman he didn't ask him "Are you a good director?" or even "Where did you work last?" but "Do you play cards?" When Hoffman replied in the negative, he was almost fired before he was hired.

At that time Shear (it was thought) was the principal villain because Ernie always played with him. But when Shear was canned and Joe Behar was in charge, Ernie found other takers. "I never played cards when I was working because that would really be defeating the whole idea," said Behar. "My idea was to get them out in the studio." Couldn't get the crew to complain, they were making triple golden time.

Behar wasn't the only one who was annoyed. Many times Edie would get dressed to go out for the night with

Ernie only to find him in the den in his shirtsleeves still at cards. "One more hand, one more hand," but she was getting no overtime.

When Irving Manesfield came west while TAGL was still his show, he and Ernie used to drive around and bet on license plates — odds or evens — "First car on the left side far corner of La Cienega and Santa Monica . . . twenty-five bucks says it's even." They kept their accounts in flux though Manesfield used to get frantic late-night calls from Ernie for small salary advances to pay off creditors or urgent gambling debts. He would also get petulant when he couldn't have his way.

When Ernie and Edie played Vegas for the periodic supper club shot, more than one hotel management prohibited him from going near the tables for fear that he'd wind up losing his whole week's salary in a night. When he couldn't play, he'd sometimes slip some money out of his vest to a friend to bet for him.

According to legend, while in Havana shooting a movie, Ernie decided to make a long distance phone call to the States. The phone booth was 15 feet from the crap tables. When he got a busy signal, he went to the tables to kill some time and wound up losing a few hundred dollars. Of course, he didn't need cards to lose money, there were far more interesting, novel ways to do it. While returning from Europe on a transatlantic liner, he once called up poor Irving in the middle of the night.

"Gotta deck of cards handy, Irving?"

"Yeah," said Manesfield groggily.

"Okay," said Ernie. "Five hundred dollars says that the first card you cut from the middle is red."

Silence . . .

"Okay, double your money . . . another five hundred dollars says it's black."

Silence . . . click. Two weeks later Ernie had a check for the full amount.

He wasn't as lucky when it came to collecting his own debts. There is one story told by Shear which seems characteristic. Once Ernie on a return trip to the Coast with a big Hollywood producer lost $8,000 in a gin game. Ernie wrote the man a check on the spot. Two weeks later up in the den, the same producer dropped four or five grand to Ernie, and then pleaded poverty. "I'm a little short right now," the man said, "I'll give you a check for a thousand." Forget it. "What are ya — crazy?" said Shear, who saw it all. "No, I don't want to do that," replied Ernie evenly.

With closer associates it was all on account to be totaled up sometime later on. At the studio he gambled for matches (split: $20; whole: $10), while in the den it was chips. These games were not the exclusive property of his more "famous" cronies either. Anyone could play — if they dared. When crew members dropped in for production meetings or whatever, Ernie always invited them to try their luck. Many declined because of the money on the table, while those who joined were flabbergasted with poker à la Kovacs. Gene Lukowsky, Ernie's TD, more or less played regularly when his budget allowed. One evening he played cards from nine at night to three in the morning. "I was over my head and I had my checkbook with me," he recalled, "and I figured, well, I can go a couple of hundred dollars. We're playing with chips, no cash involved. It turned out Milt Hoffman owed me about a hundred and a half, I owed Ernie about two bills, like that. But when we broke up, it was all for funzies, nobody paid anything. I thought if I had only known . . . I was really playing them right to the vest and unless I had a cinch I wouldn't open or stay in the pot because that was pretty big money for me. But if I had known it was all funzies, hell, I would have enjoyed the game a lot more. Nobody ever paid anybody off." Funny, Hoffman said he didn't play cards, but that must have meant on the set. Maybe he liked hanging out, maybe he was used to cigars by then — maybe Ernie just suckered him into the game.

Kovacs was pretty easy to deal with (and to), though at the time of his death there were rumors that he owed a hell of a lot from those "funzie" games. "He may have had a lot of IOU's out," said Marvin Moss, who was playing more and more gin with his client as time wore on, "but I never really knew him to hold up on the loot. With me he said, 'I'll give you a check tomorrow.' At worst it would be two days from tomorrow. I never had to chase him for money. Maybe there were guys who did, but I didn't know anybody who did." There were also rumors that Ernie was in heavy debt to high rollers in both Vegas and Miami, though they evidently never wanted the publicity.

Ern never cared whether he won or lost, he just enjoyed playing cards in any form, though enthusiasm counts for less when it comes to big money. He sometimes even won big. At a post-shower game for Jeanie Martin, Dean's fourth wife, Kovacs allegedly took a pot worth $48,000, which must have surprised the hell out of players like Dean Martin who made good money that way. Cards in any form were simply a part of his nature. Edd Henry summed it up decorously enough. "He was a high roller . . . he was a hard player. He played gin with love and determination, very serious about it all. He considered himself a champ. He was a big loser, but he was a challenger. He considered himself the best, but he wasn't, because obviously he wouldn't be losing that much if he was the best."

Part of the routine, the big, card-playing riverboat gambler with the big cigar. As an extended joke, Ernie hastily compiled a book for Doubleday in 1961 called *How to Talk at Gin*. Composed on dictabelts, and based on conversations and the conduct of people who played with him, *How to Talk at Gin* was profusely illustrated by the author. It contained a kibitzer's deathless wisdom. Under the heading "Speed of Play, Quitting the Game, and Alibis" was the following notations:

The slow player is a positive component of every gin group. There are three reasons for his being a slow player:
1. caution
2. cunning
3. stupidity

In the back he listed all his friends under various headings, great players, good players, and average players. His name was the only one in the "great" category — natch.

A card is only a card in the hands of a professional; for a comedian it's a prop. Colloquy between a journalist and a cigar smoker after the journalist has asked whether he's doing anything after the day's shooting — eating maybe?

"Then you don't play," said Mr. Kovacs, unhappily.

"Play what?"

"Poker," answered Mr. Kovacs with some derision. He added, "A poker player knows that when he's asked what he's doing at night, it really means how about a game of poker tonight?"

"I'm still available," replied the journalist.

"No, I'd feel too much like a shill if I got you into a game. If you lost you'd think I'd been trying to hook you. Knowing this, I would lose consciously. There would be no point to the game. The trick is to get people to think the game is their idea."

Instead of writing about gin, Ernie should have written an opus called *A Hustler's Guide to Poker.*

Where was it all going, all this money? Anybody's guess. The government was particularly interested in the Kovacs finances. They'd been after him since 1955 when he neglected paying his taxes while searching for his daughters. Part of the public Kovacs philosophy of finance was "I made it; it's mine," though seriously Ernie was something less of a comedian on the subject. When asked by Marie Torre, a television columnist for the late New York *Herald-Tribune,* Ernie said, "Tax is a word that causes a chill to people in show business. The tax structure has made it impossible for anyone to get excited about financial reward for creative ability. It has become necessary for the financially short-lived to incorporate to legalize his keeping a few more bucks. It's rather discouraging to realize that when the smoke blows away from the gold print on the corporate door, the professional people of today really have no desire for all these business ramifications as such. They are merely trying to hold on to some of the original money they made as boxers, actors, and singers." Hardly lines from the life of the party, the center of entertainment for the Hollywood wrecking crew.

The government hounded him incessantly nonetheless, and commenced garnishing his salaries in 1959. "It was the first time that I'd ever seen Ernie really worried about it because he realized that there was no way out of it," said Shear. "He was doing everything and anything, like fish-market openings, anything to get money to pay for the tax. He was grossing $800,000 a year, but I doubt if he was keeping a hundred — he kept going back into hock." Less funny when the government attached $90,000 of Ernie's $100,000 fee for making *Sail a Crooked Ship.*

Lemmon offered him the services of his own business manager, but after four weeks, the manager gave up. "Ernie had nine corporations and then he'd gone to Canada to get a few more like The Bazooka Doopa Hikka Hooka Hocka Company," said Lemmon, "He had it so screwed up that they [IRS] couldn't figure anything out, so they started attaching everything. They said, 'None of this can be, we can't understand it.' "

Strange? A jeep but no uniform!

Edie was more in the dark about Ernie's finances. He thought she had no business knowing about such mundane matters. She caught on soon enough. "The one thing that really got me was when finally I had to take any job that was offered to me at any price, and [Ernie] thought, 'Where are you going, what's this crap?' He didn't understand it and I didn't understand it either." While they were forcing Ernie to make pictures he didn't want to make, they were applying pressure to Edie. "The last goodie was to do the *Today Show* in New York and fly back and forth on weekends. I was supposed to do it; I had to do it. They could have even offered it to me for five hundred dollars a week." Fortunately no network is that cheap, even NBC.

Ernie fought as well as he was able, though by 1961 the tax boys were almost ready to tag his furniture to raise the cash. In a desperate move to buy time, Ernie signed away $20,000 in government bonds he'd been saving for the children. No jokes now; it was a deadly serious business of dollars and sense.

By mid-1961, there seemed to be a way out, for Ernie had finally found a business manager who could deal with his holding companies, and could offer some sound financial advice. On the day the papers announced a $75,000 income tax lien, Ernie announced the acquisition of the $2,000,000 California Racquet Club on a lease-back basis with the owner. When Edie heard the news over the phone, she reportedly told her husband, "Ernie, please try not to buy anything else until I get back."

Aside from movie money, Ernie had been trying other ploys to get himself out of hock. Publishing seemed another possible source of income and he bombarded Ken McCormick of Doubleday with an assortment of quickie book schemes. *Zoomar* had already sold 17,500 copies in the Doubleday printing by January, 1958. Kovacs actually was something of a minor literary light. In April, 1959, he started another shorter book, *John Has Fungus*, a much more personal book that cross cut between his life at home and reflections on the art of TV parody. (John, incidentally, was the name of Kippie's pet turtle who'd developed a furry growth). No dice. In June, 1960, he enthusiastically hyped his editor on another book of his own pen-and-ink drawings, and though McCormick thought they were pretty, he regretfully passed them up.

Ernie's next book proposal in December, 1960, was a compendium of the wit and wisdom of Percy Dovetonsils. "I think the book should sell awfully well," he hopefully wrote, "for these reasons: over the past eight or ten years or more actually, Percy Dovetonsils has appeared coast to coast. The mail requesting a single copy of one poem ran as high as five thousand a week at one time. After all these years there are still frequent requests each week for a picture of Percy and/or a copy of a poem." Again a regretful "no" from McCormick who thought Percy came off on TV, but in book form was less amusing.

Undaunted, Ernie commenced a far more ambitious project, a novel called *Mildred Szabo*, set in Europe during World War I. The research alone required that he read many old papers and magazines of the period. But it was so bulky to transport that eventually a few hundred pages of the manuscript were lost somewhere in transit, and the project was shelved.

Though he kept getting rejections for his quickie books, he corresponded regularly with his editor in New York. In October, 1960, after the demise of TAGL and before the Specials, he wrote to McCormick:

I have been extremely busy since I left home and have been shooting every morning and returning at seven at night. The days have all been twelve-hour ones, and while I am now only working five days a week while we were on location in London for some three and a half weeks, we were working seven days a week."

"I have another picture which I will do in June in Venice [Five Golden Hours]. *I think there is a possibility of one preceding that in April, which would be done in Sicily. When I get home, there will be a completed script waiting for me to read on a picture to be shot in January [1961] in the States. The January picture will not take as much of my time as the two pictures abroad, the latter being leads. The one in the States is one of three leads with Jack Lemmon and Debbie Reynolds. Quite honestly I am not very anxious to do the one in the States, having done this picture with the main role.*

Business was, of course, business. "It might not be a good business tactic to do lesser roles for a while. However, I am under contract to Columbia and do not have script approval."

Further on in the October, 1960, letter, Ernie talked about his Specials in characteristic haste:

When I reach home, the first thing I will have to do is quickly finish up four or five half-hour television shows so that I can tape them and leave again in the Spring [1961]. The Specials were squeezed in among Ernie's other professional commitments, but by the time he shot six of the eight in the summer of 1961, his breathless energy appeared to be on the wane. "I tape them on weekends and am done up until December now. I just finished one yesterday [August 30, 1961] and the taping sessions knock me out. I have been directing them from the control room, and the first four were done on twenty-four hour stretches. Now they're more complicated and I do them on Saturdays and Sundays . . . from six A.M. *to four* A.M. *both days.*

Memo from Scott Runge, ABC Network Production Coordinator, to Sandy Cummings. re: Special #3:

Everything short of turning off the power was done by Marvin Moss, Milt Hoffman, and myself to have Ernie carry over to next Sunday, June 4th.

My memo asking for a two-Sunday taping as such was tossed out due to Ernie's shooting schedule and acceptable only if we were to go past eleven. My suggestion on splitting the crews was not found acceptable. My efforts and the efforts of others to wind it up earlier Sunday night and carry over to next Sunday, June 4th, went down the drain. Everything possible was done to shut down, and carry over to June 4th date for taping and editing.

'Mondays and Tuesdays are kind of washouts for me as I have miserable headaches from sitting in that more or less airless room.' Milt Hoffman wasn't just complainin,' it appears."

There were also pressures which he brought on himself. With Ernie now the packager, or more accurately E&EK *Productions, Dutch Masters was giving Ernie the full price as per budget each time he delivered a completed show.* ABC *would then re-bill for their below-the-line costs, studio time, camera rental, special effects, etc. Of course, Kovacs was blowing his budget all to hell. Not that it was important right then that he was getting behind. It was more like a Mexican standoff with the studio. Any studio's dealings with any packager was summed up succinctly by one Hollywood agent: "Studios always fuck you." If you watched them all the time, maybe not, but an agent can only do so much against indices of time and space.*

They battled — agent and studio — in the gray, in the area of "ferinstance": ferinstance, when a director can't get a shot, it's the director's fault, so the packager pays. When a studio camera blows out and time's wasted finding a replacement, then the studio's at fault. Very simple? Very not so simple.

The System was curious in its simplicity; a good agent was expected to stall for his client, hold them up, hold them up in the face of threats, in the face of pleadings, make 'em wait. For example:

Letter from Milt Hoffman to Ned Tanen (MCA) *in re: Special* #2:

Enclosed you will find the final "below-the-line" billing for the Ernie Kovacs Special #1.

I have informed John Wagner, who is the comptroller for the West Coast, that E & EK *Enterprises Inc. refuses to pay the penalties for production and engineering crews for the reasons outlined in my letter. They are as follows:*
1. failure of kaleidescope which necessitated re-shooting a replacement sequence.
2. improper information as to ABC's abilities to mat correctly.
3. failure of the makeup department to follow the makeup instructions as outlined by Mr. Kovacs in the production meeting.
4. the long stage waits including the injury to ABC personnel which alone held up shooting for an hour and fifteen minutes.
5. the errors in the pre-show estimates in regard to carpenter, show onset, and carpenter show construction.

Letter from Milt Hoffman to Marvin Moss:

Enclosed please find correct billing for No. 2 Kovacs Special. As you see, this show was very heavy in construction and special effects. However, if we do not pay *the engineering penalties and production penalties, we can pull back $5,378.80, leaving a very disrespectful total of $29,556.40. I have checked this bill over and over looking for a way out, but unfortunately for us ABC made no goofs.*

Delay and obstruct, scream your agent's lungs out, "and then go in and find the obvious things where they fucked him and started screaming. I'm not saying that all those things were false", said Moss. "I used to pick up odd things and go screaming about it whenever I found one, then I'd hold up the bills. When they'd really start screaming for the money, I'd go to them and say, 'Look I really don't have the time, but I found this, I found this . . . $65 dollars.' They'd say 'we'll take it off the bill,' and I'd start to argue, 'Take 5 percent off or 10 percent off the whole bill, and I'll give you a check right now.' " Marvin was only trying to help his client. " . . . It was his money anyway, it didn't mean anything to me. I was trying to help him, and that's what I used to do."

When Ernie himself was asked about the bind, he still maintained a surface bravado, AP style, "I'll tell you why I'm a nut. I'm a nut because I'm working for nothing. Take this television show I'm putting together. The network gives me forty thousand dollars to produce a half-hour of entertainment and it is costing me fifty thousand dollars or more. Even with a tremendous turnover and volume, I've got to lose money. If I keep this up, I'll go into bankruptcy. I'm writing, directing, producing, and starring in four of these shows, but I can't afford to pay myself salaries." Ernie and the network had deducted their costs from the total package and given Ernie the difference. When they finally got around to demanding their costs, they found to their dismay that the Olive had already spent the money elsewhere.

As 1961 drew to a close, the pressure was becoming unbearable. In the midst of feverish studio activity, Ernie threw up his hands in disgust, depressed beyond measure. "I'll never get out of this," he told anyone who would listen — like Milt Hoffman or Joe Behar during those long, post-taping, sweetening sessions in the editing room. He was pushing himself beyond his own limits.

Ernie Kovacs was in danger of being another statistic in the land of tinsel dreams, but he had to show them he was good enough. He continued to hold out his own kinds of carrots to maintain his sanity, and while working, he was hustling more books for Doubleday. In the fall of 1961, he again wrote his editor, Ken McCormick, about new projects:

I will be doing a pilot for a "series." If it sells, I will be spending most of my days there and they are going to fix me up with a trailer-office so that I can work for Doubleday on the side.

And more money, an advance for his new book, *Please Excusa Da Pencil,* for 1961 sale with as large an advance as humanly possible?

Working himself into the ground and playing cards with equal intensity, Kovacs was overreaching himself. Friends were worried. A few days before his death in January, 1962, Ernie went to Dominic's to see Jack Lemmon and his wife Felicia for a drink. Lemmon noticed he was tired. "He was taping some shows and there was something in his eyes . . . very, very, strange and I remember." He remarked to his wife when Ernie had gone, "I'm terribly worried about Ernie, I really think that something terrible is going to happen."

At the last gasp, Ernie was beginning to see some relief. After taping his last special, Ernie was planning to go to New York with Edie, who was going back to Broadway in

February. At that time he was toying with the idea of directing a straight play sometime in February. In the fall he was slated to direct a Broadway musical called *Izzie and Moe*. He was also negotiating a production deal for five movies with Alec Guinness with whom he'd become good friends after they both worked in *Our Man in Havana*. They'd see eventually, and even if it wasn't in Hollywood, they'd find out soon enough.

Dutch Masters was also after Ernie to allow them to run some of his silent commercials independently of the show since they were such classics and the viewer response was overwhelming. Those residuals were looking better and better. Two days before the end, Milt Hoffman and Ernie were beginning work on some story boards for silent commercials for Colgate-Palmolive, having just received a check for development; this was another sure money maker. He wasn't too enthusiastic about that kind of commercial success, but he knew he needed the money.

January 13, 1962, started normally enough for Ernie Kovacs: bed after a late-night poker session, possibly a steam bath, or another bout with the becoming *Mildred Szabo*. He was up bright and early, hopped in his vintage white Rolls, and was off to Griffith Park for another day on the set of *A Pony for Chris*, playing a variation on his familiar Hollywood role, a snake-oil salesman in the Old West aided by his silent, Indian, sidekick Buster Keaton. At about 6:00 or 6:30 he drove over to the ABC television studios on Prospect Avenue off Hollywood Boulevard in Los Feliz to work on a sweetening session with Gene Lukowsky, where music was added and the sharp transitions between the taped bits were ironed out. By 10:00 he was finished and off again with a long night still ahead.

Later on that evening he was to meet Edie at a christening party for Milton Berle's son Michael held at Billy Wilder's house, though he still had time for a drink with his card-playing friend Joe Miklas at PJ's. After a suitable interval he proceeded on to Wilder's, pushing that heavy car down Santa Monica Boulevard toward Wilshire.

It was amazing that Ernie drove at all, considering his attitude toward driving. Whenever possible he preferred to be driven, by chauffeur or friend. Not the greatest driver by any stretch of the imagination, not wanting to be by this time; all you need a car for is to get from one place to the other, no need to get flashy. No, Ernie had passed through that love affair with car and speed, though he was always mildly amused by his cronies' excessive zeal in the pursuit of the ultimate machine. One time his friend Lemmon got an Austin-Martin as part of his income-stretching act. A few weeks later the head cracked. Ernie thought that was funnier than hell — poetic justice, tryin' to get flash.

Wilder's party wasn't spectacular — old friends, a tribal gathering. Edie had come down from the house with the new white Corvair station wagon. At Wilder's were many of Ernie's Hollywood "friends," those with whom he played cards, those who enjoyed his special humor, even some close friends who besides Wilder, Lemmon, and Quine included Lucille Ball and her new husband, Gary Morton, Berle and his wife, and Yves Montand. No press agents (unless as friends), no starlets.

Recurring flashes of familiar faces and Ernie, the kid from Trenton, with all these names, those he'd lampooned so many years before. "Hi, Ern, how's the pilot working out?" . . . "Your newest picture should be a gas" . . "Now what Ern, where's the game tonight?"

"Not tonight, fellas," or "Yeah, everything's going fine," then launching into an account of the day's events in vivid detail. It must have been increasingly difficult for Ernie to live with these demons while knowing that he was more talented. *They* were making the money. Look at their contented Hollywoodized personalities, all that showbiz behind them, and look how calm and self-assured they are. And me, what the fuck am I doing, why can't I get a chance . . . what's the use of knowing Wilder if he won't let me do something great . . . yet he comes to my house . . . why, why? Look, Ernie, you're not top box-office material, you've got a mustache and you look too ethnic for those dramatic roles. Stick with these parts and at least you'll work — you'll have work as long as you live. You'll have parts as long as you live . . .

Being under all that hair and cigar smoke and essentially a shy man, Ernie overcompensated among his immediate "peers," reverting to type — the life of the party, miles and miles away from his den, his kingdom.

Comedian Gary Morton who attended the christening with his recent bride, Lucille Ball, recalled: Ernie was in great form at the party. He had just finished this Western pilot and was in high spirits. He described vividly and with great wit and humor his experiences. The Kovacs cigar was in great evidence. Ernie told how cold it was on location for the pilot film and recounted — as only he could — his experiences when they told him to take his shirt off. He rocked us with laughter describing how shivery he was. It was, of course, a very warm occasion, and Ernie added the warmth that only he could add.

— Item from AP story, Philadelphia *Inquirer,* Jan. 13, 1962

For Kovacs it was the same old movie in the land of movie shades in costume and prop — life of the party, being himself or whatever approximation he manifested, with his "friends" of five years' standing. Five years, and he still had a case of the syndrome. Eugene in script-city without a script. His "friends" had the monopoly. Popular in the popular eye . . . be damned. At least he wrote his own material which is more than he could say for Berle.

Wilder and Lemmon understood, but what could they do? They were successful in spite of the system but I'm the misfit, the accepted misfit, the kook . . .

Living in Hollywood was like being one step from Forest Lawn with a press-release funeral in the background, vistas of the aimless wandering between Dominic's, PJ's, or the Villa Capri. Ernie Kovacs had sworn off gambling again by January, 1962:

Edie and I returned to Vegas this morning . . . This is a town I really loathe . . . I don't gamble there anymore and I still loathe it.

— Letter to McCormick

Hollywood had become the dead end. The pot of gold contained taxmen and their clipboards. Fuck 'em, I earned the money, I'll keep it, just see if you can get your fucking hands on it you bastards . . . so, I'll sign over the bonds (get some time to figger a way to stop them) . . .

. . . but *they* come to me in the den, my den, they all come and we have a great time shooting the shit and playing cards and there's no one around to bother us. Maybe I'll finish *Mildred Szabo* and sell it to Ken for some bucks, need some *bucks*, need some real work . . . anything. Okay, I'll go to New York and take that play, whatever in hell it is, make it into something, the ole Kovacs touch. Also I'll keep an eye on Edie, keep those men from slobbering all over her. Jeez what am I gonna do about this fucking mess? . . .

This party's a goddamn tape loop . . . Howareya, Milton, congrats. Here's something for the kid . . . hope he'll use it well . . . hope you can keep up the payments . . . boy!

It's like a party in Trenton when you put the lights out, only here they write press releases . . . vision of the reality of the dream . . . the "Rat Pack" . . . jeez with agent variations:

Ernie tried to get into the Hollywood scene, it was important to him. And he was socially accepted by the group that was active at the time . . . The Rat Pack, the Wilders, the whole thing of being invited to those parties and so forth . . . and he was invited, he did get to meet those people and they did like him.

Yes, Marvin, pray continue the vision — Ernie in Kovacsland? Hardly:

If the Rat Pack existed, Ernie was, if not in it, on the edge. He was close to it, he wasn't really in it I would say, but he was close to it —

Sez E: *Outside of a brief association I once had with a fraternal organization (which I joined mostly because they had slot-machines in back), I have always had an antipathy to organizations. The members of the Rat Pack are, individually, good friends of mine and Edie's. However, nothing would embarrass me more, personally, than to think I was a member of a little group. This would eventually lead to our all wearing identical beanies with "Rat Pack" on the front and a local tavern sponsor on the back of our sweat shirts. I've never been much of an advocate of "Hey fellows, let's go in for a swim" type of existence and neither has Edie. I would hate to go into my old age greeting friends with a secret handshake.*

The agent continues "Jeanie Martin gave this party and I was invited but that wasn't my regular group, I was impressed I will admit. I walk in and here standing around the bar is Dean, Frank, Milton Berle, Shirley MacLaine, and Lemmon. Milton Berle got up and gave ten minutes of stale jokes, the worst, the same thing as the guy in West Covina who would have put a lamp shade on his head, no better. Dean finally said, "Oh fuck this, Milton," and they started a poker game. I wasn't about to get into that poker game. It was one of the dullest evenings I've ever spent in my whole life.'

"When I went down with the bloody cigars, it was so awful and bizarre because there he was. They had dressed him all up, and this pimply-faced kid is there, saying, 'We're terribly *proud of the job we've done . . . I think he looks marvy . . . I assume it will be open?' and I said, 'No, it's gonna be closed.' 'Oh,' and he's just looking at Ernie and beaming at his work. Now I go to put the cigars in, but I can't open it up [the pocket]. It's tight because the clothes are form fitting. He's got it pulled in the back and everything else. I'm trying to get the cigars in the pocket and I'm thinking, 'Holy Jesus and now they're flaking all over the place.' The pimply-faced attendant is going berserk. It was so bizarre and awful, and then I started to laugh because what else can you do? I said, 'I can't believe this is happening.' I might have known it would happen like that 'cause I know he was circling overhead and laughing his ass off.' "*

Ernie left the party at one o'clock after bidding adieus. He was going back to PJ's for a nightcap with Miklas, then home for some work.

Seconds later, a young man who'd witnessed the accident pulled up to the intersection. He's seen Ernie on television and driving around Beverly Hills. There was nothing he could do now. Dick Quine, also at Wilder's and one of Ernie's directors, pulled up shortly thereafter. A crowd formed, then the police moved in while the news flashed throughout the community. Quine immediately called Edd Henry who left for Ernie's house to break the news to Edie. Refusing to believe him, she asked Jack Lemmon to go down to the morgue to verify the gruesome truth. Only then did Edie break down.

By Sunday morning the crowds of the curious were besieging the Kovacs household on Coldwater Canyon Road, jostling each other like the mobs in the movie premier scene from Nathanial West's *Day of the Locust.* A Beverly Hills detective, with whom Ernie used to ride on patrol duty from time to time, tried to control the mob until Marvin Moss and PR man Henri Bollinger took charge, sorting the friends from the ghoulish.

After the gruesome truth was revealed, and funeral arrangements were made, Ernie was still our ironic soul, even in repose. As a favor to Edie, Lemmon went down to the funeral parlor to put some cigars in Ernie's pockets as a last sentimental gesture. Lemmon in Kovacsland?

Ernie's funeral was a Hollywood event of rare import. Many stars Ernie knew personally and many he didn't know, that Edie thought should come, paid tribute. The agents oversaw the invited guests at the church of which Ernie was nominally a member, just a few blocks from the scene of the accident. The regular minister was out of town and his assistant was called in for the eulogy. Edie thought that would save needless bickering among his friends. The minister's assistant read a poem by Edgar A. Guest called "Somebody Said It Couldn't Be Done," a saccharine piece of doggerel, ". . . for Ernie Kovacs, one of the most original, bright writers and performers and directors that we have ever known," Lemmon remarked.

"Now I want to tell you, Ernie must have been buzzing overhead in hysterics; there's no way he wasn't," said Lemmon. Percy Dovetonsils maybe, not Edgar Guest. Whatta finale, carried to the final reward by Lemmon, Sinatra, Joe Miklas, Dean Martin, and Ernie's brother, Tom. Edward G. Robinson, George Burns, Jack Benny, Kim Novak, Danny Thomas, Sam Goldwyn, Jimmy Stewart — all of them were there, for they respected his shade.

Joe Behar, Ernie's first director, was there with the famous and caught the irony of it all. "Those funerals . . . I've never been a funeral celebrity. You go there and it's so funny. They got two agents from MCA who stand at the front door and make sure that everybody who goes in there knew him, but it's so funny to see two agents, two sharpies from MCA standing there kind of screening everybody as they go in. It's almost like when he was alive and they did that, after he's dead they're still representing him."

Moss recalls, "I remember at the funeral there was me, I think Joe Miklas, and somebody else who we figured between the three of us knew everybody that Ernie knew, and we stood by the door of the church to decide who would get in and who wouldn't. But it wasn't a scene at the church, it was very interesting. A lot of tourists showed up but they stayed outside; they didn't try to get in."

Ernie Kovacs was buried at Forest Lawn Cemetray in the Hollywood Hills. "Ernie Kovacs 1919-1962 Nothing in Moderation" read the epitaph on his simple stone. "He was one of those nuts who got to know everybody and everybody loved him," said friend Lemmon in tribute. Not only did they mourn him in Hollywood, but wherever thre were people who loved to laugh and use their vision as Kovacs had, a vision where freedom was paramount, the freedom to laugh the cosmic laugh — one more time.

Ernie's death released a torrent of condolences not only from people in the immediate community, but newspaper reporters and radio journalists throughout the country. The press agents had a difficult time screening the sympathetic from the ghoulish curiosity seekers. Weeks afterward, the second wave hit. Even dying didn't extricate Kovacs from his financial problems. The days, weeks, months, and years afterward were almost nightmarish ones for Edie, Kippie, Bette, and Mia Susan born in 1959. At the time of his death, Ernie's estate was valued at well over $2,000,000, though there was approximately $7,000 in ready assets (as opposed to claims of well over $150,000) before Ernie's shadows, the Internal Revenue Service had their shot. Besides claims to $71,628 for overdue payments in 1959, the IRS filed a second lien against the estate for an additional $130,165.47 for Ernie's failure to pay income tax in 1956 57 — a cool $200,000.

Two and a half weeks after the accident, ABC also filed against the estate for $220,632 claiming that E&EK Productions failed to pay them for the accumulated "below-the-line" costs of stage managers, technical directors, film editors, etc., though they were willing to settle for 7 percent of the total monies owed. ABC really had no thought of collecting the money; they merely wanted to establish tax credit to deduct the debt themselves and suing the estate assured their tax loss. The System was indeed wreaking its revenge.

Ernie's friends offered to do a benefit for Edie and her family but she graciously turned them down, even though she was now fighting for her life, her children's existence, and her house. The vultures had descended. Ernie's first wife, Bette, came from Florida to lay claim to both Ernie's estate as his legal wife (Mexican marriage was contested) and custody of Kippie and Bette. After a messy and quite sensational public hearing and trial, her claim was disallowed, and the children remained with their stepmother. A year later, Mary Kovacs, Ernie's outspoken mother, who never really liked Edie, anyway, accused her of mismanaging Ernie's estate and being an unfit mother. She petitioned the courts for control of the assets and the children. Ironically enough she had testified against Bette in the previous year's custody battle.

Mary also accused Edie of withholding monies due her from insurance policies Ernie supposedly took out in her name. However there was no policy for her and never had been. Undoubtedly he'd meant to, but instead the insurance went to his children and was underwritten in such a manner that neither the government nor ABC could attach it for themselves. Mary went to court in 1966 and lost. He'd paid rent on her apartment on Hollywood Boulevard and provided her with a car. No more could he do. The pot at the end of the Hollywood rainbow was tapped out.

Ernie's death thrust his sheltered wife into the unwelcomed light of the most lurid publicity. Not only did she successfully defend her position as mother and executor of his legacy, but she also subsequently prospered herself. Through her own diligent work and a few courses at UCLA, she mastered the intricacies of Ernie's tax debauch, and paid off all his outstanding debts.

I've never had quite the same thing happen with other people, that passed away, where the memory is so indelible that you forget sometimes that they're gone. A year or year and a half later they are still indelible in your mind and you still think about them. Several times I got caught literally and I couldn't believe myself. I'd suddenly say when somebody was talking, "Oh shit, that's wonderful, wait until Ernie hears it . . ." I'd forget. He was still there. He really left a mark; he wasn't just a talented nice guy.

— Jack Lemmon

It still impresses me that you want to write the book because it just seems so hard for me to believe that other people feel the same way I do. He was really like my personal friend and nobody else had him as a friend, yet I know the other guys had him as friend. Somehow he seemed special to us; he was our special friend.

— Bob Kemp, ABC cameraman

After you worked with him, you could work for years and they all looked like babies.

— Barbara Murphy, wardrobe mistress, *Take a Good Look*

I couldn't smoke the last cigar he gave me. I just couldn't smoke that big Cuban thing. It finally died in the refrigerator; it just fell apart. I couldn't smoke it really. Isn't that weird? I should have had a Jack Daniels and smoked it.

— Bob Haley, ABC cameraman

It's been more than a decade since Ernie wrapped himself around a phone pole on Santa Monica Boulevard, yet the boys on the back lot still remember him.

One legendary party Ernie hosted for his ABC crew at the Villa Capri cost him $5,000. He came up to Bob Haley during the melee and deliriously exhorted him, "Hey, Bob, go around and tell everybody to drink triple martinis. Drink, drink the best cognac. Go throw up, come back and drink more, get sick, drink more. That way word will get around Hollywood that not only do I drink, but my friends drink, too."

Haley organized a party for Ernie and Edie one Christmas by soliciting $10 from each of the crew which amounted to $600 or $700. With tears in his eyes Ernie exclaimed, "It's the best party I've been to in five days of partying." "And it was a really neat party because the people that worked with him threw it," remarked Bob. "It's a rarity for that to happen in Hollywood. It *does* happen, Steve Allen throws a party once in a while. I'm not saying it doesn't happen, but very rarely when you're a technician."

"The parties were unbelievable," adds Kemp, "it was a first-class arrangement, all first class. We've had a lot of parties around here, but I guess his parties have been just about the best. The big parties were off the lot. They were for wives, husbands, boyfriends, girlfriends, whatever. It wasn't like he was a big Hollywood star and you were sitting there at his party. We were just having a party." All that plus overtime, and it wasn't even work.

"It didn't matter what you did. You could be as creative as you wanted," reiterates Haley jovially. "Every week you looked forward to doing the show and after twenty-four hours you hated to go home. Now that's never happened in television. It's like a party, a total trip. Off camera it was still a party. 'Come on up to the house and play some cards anytime boys.' "

Ernie like to give away bottles. "I used to go up to the house anytime I wanted to. I was welcome, Haley said. "I used to take advantage of it... not too much. I didn't want to go there and drink all his wine, which I would have." Haley used to get a case of wine every so often with notes. "Here are six bottles, I want you to let me know what it's like, and these six bottles, just enjoy."

The freewheeling spirit generated on set manifested itself in practical jokes, mostly at the expense of poor Percy, a perennial favorite of the Kovacs crews. Once back at NBC, Shear decided to slip Dovetonsils a mickey. "We knew damn well he never had any breakfast," said Perry Cross, co-conspirator and producer, "and he probably didn't have dinner, and he wrote all night." Percy was a tippler and liked to have a deep-dish martini handy for moral courage when reading. One morning 2 1/2 ounces of tequila was substituted. When Ernie gulped it down as per script, he was instantly smashed on the set, rooted to his chair. Partially putting on the guys and mostly because he was really leveled, he sat in his armchair for the remainder of the show emitting drunken "umphs," tears streaming from beneath his cross-eyed glasses. On another occasion someone put a goldfish in Percy's glass.

For whatever reasons, Ernie thought Perry was responsible for all the on-set nonsense. At that time Perry worked the floor while Shear caught the angles in the booth. Coming back from a commercial break after doing his "Superclod" bit, Ernie disappeared. Barry yelled at Perry to get on camera quick, "Do something!!" Cross confronted the perplexed studio audience lamely, "Ladies and Gentlemen, there seems to be something wrong," desperately ad libbing on camera with no Ernie and no Edie in sight! Suddenly, Edie popped up from nowhere and announced, "This is our producer, a very talented man," and then the Archy Cody Trio struck up "Slippin' and a Slidin'," a rock and roll tune which Perry had mocked to Ernie some time ago. "Now the audience, I'm sure, didn't know what the hell was going on," Perry later said, "but Ernie had this high-pitched laugh. I could hear him laughing down the hall. I could have killed him."

Besides the famous Percy substitution, the boys at ABC pulled another switcheroo, Jack Daniels for gin. Percy pursed his lips, sipped and lisped, "Hmm . . . whoever thought of brown gin?" "I almost fell off my camera," said Haley, "because what is a guy going to say? There's no other way to explain why it's brown."

Ernie's humor was never for everyone. "He was for himself," recalled Bob Kemp, "he really didn't care about the people at home. He was losing money on the show — but Ernie wouldn't compromise. You see he was striving for his artistic point. It was terribly important to him. It didn't matter what the network thought; it didn't matter what the people at home thought; he had to do it his way — and he did it great." [The ratings weren't great? — ed.]

"*The Kovacs Show* never had good ratings," said Moss. "Fuck that, Ernie Kovacs sold Dutch Masters cigars. That was the ballgame; that's what Mogulescu cared about and rightfully so. He didn't give a shit what the rating was." Kovacs was an acquired taste anyway.

He bridled in his vision against the specious rationality of cost accountants and the 12-year-old mentalities of the sponsors who were wasting a creative medium while executives temporized. At the time, Robert Kitner, former president of NBC in the late Fifties, saw some of the problem, "I think all the networks have balanced programming which we know a great bulk of the people in this country do not particularly care for." Peter Leavathes, former president of Twentieth Century Fox Television, made a far blunter statement, "You've got to look at television realistically, as what it is today [1960]. The sponsor buys a show to sell his product. That is the basic purpose of TV. To sell someone's product. To do that you've got to be entertaining. A sponsor doesn't care in most cases how you sell his wares."

Networks explained and explained to Congress, which at the time was investigating the rigging of the then popular quiz shows *21* and *The $64,000 Question,* how sponsors had coached children in cheating while the sales of Geritol boomed. That's entertainment? For whom? Why, the lady from Cincinnati, of course, a woman who according to an unpublished Kovacs article for *Life,* " . . . makes a list of all the commercial products sold. Frantically switching back and forth among the three stations so as not to miss any of the commercial announcements, she prefers flashy ads to guest stars, and would object if they were cut down in time or volume." All programming was geared toward this mythical creature (part housewife, part hooker). He concludes with some reasoning, "If there is something to the conception of 'the woman from Cincinnati,' then the clothing industry could simplify its production by manufacturing just one fabric and one design in one size."

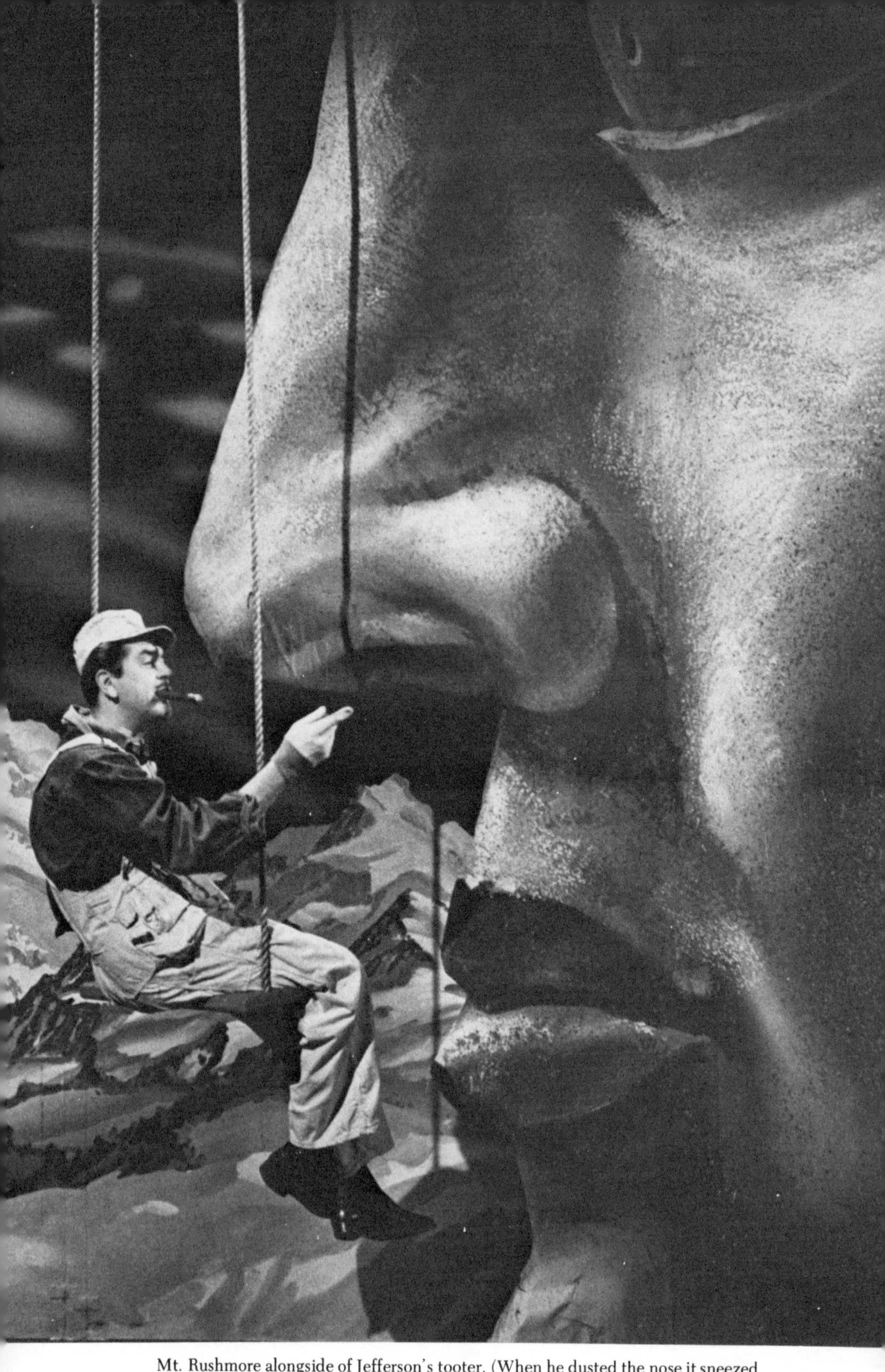

Mt. Rushmore alongside of Jefferson's tooter. (When he dusted the nose it sneezed and blew Ernie away)

In the 1957 draft of the article, he talked about the never-ending parade of misery-billed-as-entertainment quiz shows. He had good reason for once, telling Barbara Murphy, "Don't watch too much television because it will only clutter your mind."

He brought the vision to television. Said Haley munching imaginary popcorn while expostulating, stuffing the whole box into his mouth, transfixed, "He wanted people to sit, he was trying to educate on all his shows for the subtle quiet humor, the 'hah hah' instead of the 'hahahaha.' He wanted people to watch the screen at all times. You had to watch it like in the movies."

Wonder is a pie in the face, or the White Rock Girl taking a bath. Ernie loved his pies and on occasion got carried away. During an NBC morning extravaganza production of "By the Sea" complete with gay nineties costumes and a pie vendor selling his wares, the spontaneous vision overtook the script. While Edie was thrushing, Ernie went to purchase a pie from vendor Wendell whose crooked pie arm met the Kovacs kisser. Wendell ducked Ernie's return shot and a meringue free-for-all commenced. One sent Edie sprawling into 15 inches of goo. Meanwhile Kovacs and Bill ran back to the lockers for more ammunition. Then Ernie with four pies on his broad arms turned to Bill. "I've got mine," he gleefully said. By the finale not only was the entire cast covered with pie, but also the producer, the director, most of the cameramen, and the band. Ernie wound up paying for one trumpet and replacing the watch of one member of the chorus which he, of course, suitably inscribed.

Inscription was a big thing with Ernie. He once got into hot water with a top executive from NBC for giving Shirley Mellner a credit on a Special. Assistant producers never get credit, said the executive from his molehill, everyone else will want one — besides it's against company rules.

"But she's always gotten Associate or Assistant Producer, that's her credit," Ernie said. The executive wasn't impressed. Kovacs was adamant, "Well then, there'll be no credits," said the Brass. Shirl told him to forget it, the show was more important.

When the show was finally aired a few weeks later, Ernie as per usual gave a small party for the staff. Ernie gave Shirley a gold charm bracelet with a heart and a loving cup. Over the heart was engraved "Assistant Producer," and on the back of the loving cup "Screw Hal Kemp."

Actually, Ernie commemorated many occasions with style, even occasions when he had to admit he was wrong. When Milt Hoffman fired one of Ernie's staff, he was mad enough to try to have Hoffman canned. Eventually Hoffman proved himself right. Ernie woke up at four in the morning to tell him so, and then sent him a pair of gold cufflinks which were inscribed, "Where the fuck is . . . Peggy?"

As for language, Ernie swore with love and abandon. Hoffman once hired a secretary and the first time Ernie spied her, he said, "Baby, I'd like to fuck you." Not that uncommon a statement in Hollywood, land of the creamy thigh. The lady ran to Milt who explained, "If Ernie didn't like you he wouldn't be able to say that to you . . . and he only talks dirty to people he likes." No further problems.

Marianne Hooper, one of Ernie's production assistants at ABC, now a producer for NBC, recalled similar circumstances, "He was volatile. He used to cuss a lot in the booth and it was funny the first time I was in the booth, he turned around and said, 'Excuse me.' It was so much a part of him. Since I was new he wanted to make sure I wasn't offended — it just shows his sensitivity."

He could also be a frequent recipient of raspberries from his crews. "With Ernie it didn't matter what you said to him," said Kemp, "one day I said, 'Fuck you, Ernie.' I just got pissed off at him. I could say that to him, and it would go at that. I couldn't think of saying that to Sinatra."

In an atmosphere free of rules, Kovacs and his boys created masterpieces. All one had to give was interest, love, and dedication.

I've worked on two shows that were creative . . . Garroway and Kovacs. They were truly creative shows from my standpoint because I could do my expression with my camera. What you put down was yours. No one told me what to put down. Usually it's one or two cameramen who do the show, but in this case it was all the cameramen, three or four guys and me.

— Bob Haley

The highpoint of everyone's career on the ABC lot was working for the Olive:

I've done 10,000 television shows and I'll tell you that the Kovacs show was one of the best . . . and The Julie Andrews Show. *I always think of the Kovacs show as being one of the best. I've got a big picture of Ernie, a 16 x 20 of Percy Dovetonsils, in my study and I just enjoy looking at it. I also have a letter that Ernie sent me which says something like 'Thanks.' The Emmys I got for the show are great, yet the Emmy doesn't mean as much to me for* The Ernie Kovacs Show *as it does for* The Julie Andrews Show. The Julie Andrews Show *I did and created what I hoped would get me the Emmy. On the Kovacs show, Ernie did it. Ernie created this monstrosity that turned out to be a great thing that people loved, and we won the Emmy for it, but Ernie really gets the credit for that.*

— Bob Kemp

Ernie possessed the spontaneous vision of a child in his grown-up little boy's room, and it was this child his Hollywood companions loved so much. If his advisors understood, they did so grudgingly. When he was supposed to be working on a script, Moss caught him building a balsamwood replica of the new wing to be added on to the den. "Ferchrissakes, that's what you have architects for," he said. Ernie smiled and continued his infinitely more important project, his playpen.

Ernie had an innocent enthusiasm for people. At first introduction he immediately wanted to include you in his activities, whether it was cigars, cards, or steam baths. He was open to giving of himself spontaneously. He was copied unmercifully by other comedians who never really understood just how free his laughter was. Close friends tried to protect him. "He was an easy mark and everybody picked his brain, took advantage of him, stole him blind," said Barry Shear. "It would just make his friends sick to watch, but Kovacs was too nice a guy to complain. Most of the unnice people he met, he met out here because this is a town which cuts you apart."

Innocence prevailed. At the time of his death Ernie was thinking about expanding Eugene into a full-length movie. Eugene was the *schlemiel,* the poor schnook who looked on, astonished at the incongruities of modern life, a character to whom things happened, a character who searched for wonder — status kissing, doorknobs falling, tables and worlds tilting. Eugene was a character born from life — Kovacs without the big cigar, the big car, and the turntable in the driveway. Eugene was most memorable because he was without pretentions.

Kovacs was in control of his own myth. Marc Connelly in his late 70s, a gentle survivor of a more elegant literary age and a good friend from New York, called him "blithe" like his own associates of the Twenties and Thirties. "I remember the color of Ernie, the nimbus around him. I remember it was so three-dimensional. Ernie had practically no echoes in him — a dear preposterous son-of-a-gun. He erupted as much as he wrote. His laughter was generous laughter."

With all his generosity and good nature, he was intolerant only of The Rules, be they the rules of sponsors, network executives who attempted to censor his creations, the government which harried him to death, or even the hallowed and restricted New York Athletic Club. When Ernie was living in New York and a member of the Club, he decided to invite Shear and Cross over for a steam bath after work. "We can't go in there," they said, "we're both Jewish. They won't have us as members." Ernie said he'd take care of it, "I won't go in there unless you come with me." The Club couldn't refuse Ernie and they were his guests several times. "Just be sure when you walk out of the steam room you carry a towel in front of you, so they won't know you're Jewish," he joked. Though he made light of the incident, he was extremely concerned. No organization was too austere, no rules so inflexible that they couldn't be bent for his friends.

Pretension in any form drew his wrath, albeit comically. When he was still new to Hollywood ways he went to a party with Shirley Mellner at the Bel-Aire mansion of William Getz, a producer who (unbeknown to Ernie) happened to be a well-known art collector. They drove up to the huge mansion with its imposing three-story-high front door and were greeted by a Japanese houseboy. (Ernie just finished remarking to Shirl, "Wanna bet they have a Japanese houseboy?" Shirl was already giggling.) Getz greeted them after being introduced by Sinatra, who was leaving to attend a benefit. The host ushered them into a huge living room with beautiful paintings on the walls. Bill and the rest of the party sat down on a couch along the wall while Ern and Shirley occupied two commodious easy chairs in front of the sofa. The lights dimmed, the drapes parted, and down came a movie screen covering the paintings. It was movietime in Bel-Aire, a local custom which neither of the honored guests was familiar with.

While the credits for an Alfred Hitchcock movie were flashing, both were sinking into the plush of the chairs, trying to stifle their giggles at all this pomp and circumstance. After ten minutes passed, Getz solicitously came over to them, "You don't like this? You've seen it? Okay?" Presto! On came June Allyson and Jimmy Stewart in *Strategic Air Command,* which made them giggle more. Finally Ernie excused himself to make a phone call, and when he returned he urged Shirley to do the same. "But I don't have to make a phone call," she protested. "Just do it."

Over the table where the phone sat was Van Gogh's *Self-Portrait,* the original. They both realized that all the pictures on the walls were equally as real. It was all too silly for words, they'd both had enough. "Are you ready to leave?" "You had it?" he asked Shirl. They approached Getz and Ernie asked seriously, "Excuse me, Mister Getz, but do you have any UPA cartoons?" No, said Getz. "Well," Ernie replied deadpan, "we'll have to leave."

After being ushered out by the Japanese houseboy and seated on the steps in front of the imposing three-story doors, they erupted hysterically at what they'd seen and done.

Getz and Kovacs soon became friends, and Getz wound up playing cards in the den like everyone else in Hollywood that Ernie met. His circle wasn't strictly limited to those few with the million-dollar smiles and reputations. Ernie made no differentiations among friends. One of those people who was indispensable to Moss, Edd Henry and Edie in those grim days after the accident was a detective from the Beverly Hills police force with whom Ernie used to cruise on occasion, a friend whom Lemmon had known about through Ernie but had never met. Ernie was used to riding around in patrol cars. He still had some good friends on the Trenton force, Detective Anthony Raywood and Fred Hutchinson, the two patrolmen who chased down his first wife in Newark. At his death he was still in contact with Van Kirk, his old dramatics coach. "Ernie," said Lemmon, "was a shotgun instead of a bullet. He was into all kinds of different relationships with people."

Actually, he enlarged his circle as he went along, and the television viewer was privileged to see it all. People still remember Kovacs and his stunts in Trenton. Some say he still haunts the fog-shrouded streets of downtown Trenton, wrapped in his opera cape. Say the name Kovacs in Philadelphia, eyes light up, smiles form. New York City still has a soft spot for Harvey, the World's Strongest Ant. With his death an era was ended but his boys were loyal to him throughout. When Andy McKay contacted Trig Lund with the news he was down in San Diego. Trig drove directly to Coldwater Canyon to see what he could do for Edie. Haley was in a bar in Pebble Beach when a newspaper was mysteriously shoved under his nose. He saw the headlines, "Ernie Kovacs TV Star Killed in Crash." He continued drinking for eight solid hours. Then he drove to a motel and called Edie.

Shirley Mellner was so broken up that she was a wreck for weeks and never even made the funeral. Gene Lukowsky cried. He'd worked with Ernie just a few hours before his death in a sweetening session for an upcoming Special. "I couldn't believe it, it can't be true, it can't be. A president is assassinated, people tend to believe it. But with Ernie, no one wanted to believe it, it couldn't have happened. It was a bad thing for us."

Ernie's still around if you speak with Perry Cross:

We were sitting in a restaurant about two years ago [1971]. Ernie came up in the conversation while subconsciously we started to hear music coming out of the Muzak. Of all things to hear, it was Solfeggio. *Suddenly Barry [Shear] said "Hold it . . . " Beyond coincidence, it was more like somebody was saying, "Hey guys, I know you're talking about me." It took me about three days to get over that.*

One knows instinctively that wherever Ernie is at this moment, there is a game in progress with plenty of Havanas, and fountains of Jack Daniels and Wild Turkey. Sky's the bottom line. It's a good game now, Aristophanes, Ben Jonson, Petronius, Ernie, and Molière. It's been quite a heavy game. Jonson is trying to sucker Ernie into betting. Ernie's got a pair of threes. "Raise ya Ben, just to keep ya honest," he smirks behind his mustache. Meanwhile Sam Goldwyn, Max Sennett, and Harry Cohn mosey over to kibbitz. Molière has already told Ern that he didn't consider his performance in *L'Avare* hammiest in the least. Jonson agrees.

Maybe not, maybe there's just this huge control room where Ernie is taping, up to his eyes in monitors. He's not laughing exactly, he's sort of smiling; and it was all for real.

Kemp summed it up: "He would do a skit and it would be funny, but he was serious about it. We all laughed, but it was a serious thing to him who wanted to make us laugh."

College students can see *Kovacs*, a documentary sponsored by the Dutch Masters Company compiled by Jack Mogulescu and Terry Galleny, which contains bits from *Take a Good Look* and the Specials representing two years out of a possible twelve. As for the rest, Dumont destroyed all their kinescopes during an economy drive a few years back. NBC has some of theirs salted away in a warehouse in New Jersey or upstate New York. It would cost a fortune to track them down, much less view them. CBS, WPTZ, and WTTM have snippets, while the audio portions of Ernie's shows from 1952 to 1954 from Dumont and CBS

Goldy Locks

reside in the Kovacs Archives deep in the vaults of UCLA's special collection, containing over 200 lp's. Luckily, the Museum of Broadcasting in New York City has a fine representative collection of Kovacs shows. But the parties remain alive in the memories of his friends.

Insert for "Kovacs on Music" from the original script entitled "Cartoon", May 22, 1959.

The idea, as I explained on the phone, is something Edie has wanted to do for a long time. I once did a thing in Phillie where I was electronically matted into an old Karloff Film. We necessarily has [sic] to put me in dark areas in this, but the thing worked quite well. This one, of course, will be much better. I imagine there will be a little trouble around neckline matchings. There will be two figures cartooned and animated, without heads, so that Edie's and my head can be inserted into these spots camera-wise. This sheet might only be a one-and-a-half-minute-type thing..

I think the neckline might best be white. The neck would be all animation and the only thing supplied is the head by the live cameras. I think the joining of the head and animation will be easier if the outside edges of the neck aren't matched . . . I must apologize for what seems like a great deal of reiteration, but working through the mail like this, I want to be sure. Let us say we start the whole thing this way:

A figure of a girl in a cowgirl outfit (this and opening should make this, all in all, approximately a two-and-a-half or three-minute bit) and a figure of a man in cowboy outfit enter. They do not have heads. The girl opens a small box and takes out a folded guitar which she snaps out larger than the box, conceivable, in happy cartoonland. Then male figure going rapidly through his pockets, pulls out small balloon-type thing which he blows up and becomes a bass. He stamps his foot, one and two and one and two, then with gesture prevents guitar player from beginning, exits, and returns with two boxes marked his and hers. They open the boxes and each puts on a head (cartoon but as photographically realistic as possible of Kovacs and Adams, facing front, with eyes closed). He puts Kovacs head on girl's body and Edie's on his. She feels above her (no cigar in Kovacs mouth . . . in drawing). There is a white cowboy hat on each. These hats will have to be copied from the costume department. Ask Marvin Moss at MCA to please have wardrobe immediately; get those two hats so that you can duplicate them in your drawing. My size 7 3/8, ask Mary to get Edie to give him hers.

Correction: Edie's facing front, I will face rear. Kovacs figure puts up hand, feels Edie's face and hair, snaps finger at Edie's figure and they change places, taking their instruments with them. After check if proper head is in place, discovers that his head is on backwards by feeling in hair while searching for nose, puts up both hands, turns around facing front. He does this too quickly and head starts to slip off, so he straightens it. After this, both figures slap the sides of their own faces vigorously and here is where you take out both heads and camera will put our live heads. We slowly open eyes and note we have live heads with cartoon bodies. (After slapping process the figures are drawn without heads unless otherwise noted.) While this has taken two hours to read, from the beginning to this point should not be too long . . . perhaps a half a minute, or at most 45 seconds. Now we begin with Kovacs figure beating time with foot to begin song. He stomps a one and two and a one and two, and they begin playing. Kovacs figure points off right, we will hear an "A" on the piano. Then he tries, gets a clinker. "A" will sound three or four times more impatiently and firmly until he tunes to position.

Try to do this in positive movements inasmuch as head movements by Kovacs will have to be synched with this action. Costumewise, the two figures' clothing should have humor, perhaps a big gun that weighs heavily on one side and tends to pull trousers down a bit so that Kovacs figure hikes it up now and then, perhaps on Edie's figure, a gun belt that is two [sic] large and whole thing begins sliding down over skirt and she occasionally pulls up. Actually this same device should not be used on both . . . something different for Edie. And even so, the less number of times this happens, the better unless something really funny can be developed. After Kovacs stomps the one and a two, one and a two, Edie begins singing:

When I was young I used to wait
On my master and give him his plate,
and pass the bottle when he got dry,
and brush away the blue-tail fly . . .

(We immediately hear shrill whistle) Kovacs and Edie stop playing and look (physically live, that is) down to the lower left (camera right) frame. In walks a blue-tail fly wearing white tie, top hat, and tails. Somehow we indicate (even though we are in black and white) that the tails are blue. He is wearing white gloves and carrying cane. He gestures and two flies in stagehands outfits, hammers hooked in belt, come rushing in and plant in the center large pitcher of buttermilk. One runs off, returns quickly with a bag of peanuts which he empties into buttermilk. Valet replaces these two and helps formally dressed fly to remove his tails, etc., leaving him in bathing trunks with blue round spot on rear. *(NOTE: After we establish formally coated blue-tail fly on whistle and we see Edie and Ernie look down, we will until indicated. Now use a drawing only of lower section of legs and possibly hips of two drawn figures so that we can see the action of the buttermilk business closer. A script for camera will be prepared for this film and here the indication will be for camera to take out faces.) After fly props are set and the valet leaves, he snaps finger and we hear Edie and Ernie sing, but do not see them except lower extremities.)*

Flies in the buttermilk goober peas,
Flies in the buttermilk goober peas,
Flies in the buttermilk goober peas.

During the singing, the fly runs center takes a quick bow, jumps in the buttermilk at the "flies in the buttermilk" line and pulls out two peanuts from the buttermilk on each "goober peas" line. Immediately after the last line, he flies to his original spot which is quickly set up with a folding director's chair by the little fly stagehand and sits down.

(There is a stop in the music while he does this, but it must be done very quickly).

He then gestures royally up toward us and we return to the original wide shot.
(NOTE: In the script for camera, it will not be indicated Kovacs and Edie in.)

Edie sings:

I know an old lady, who swallowed a fly . . .

(c. u. fly who does a tremendous take and dashes behind chair. Script: Kovacs and Edie out. Edie sings off camera: "perhaps she'll die.")

For this line, we either have the fly looking very pleased that the woman will die or sneering at the assumption that a fly could kill her. Which ever look comes off best. Or perhaps we have him sneering and looking tough at the thought he could kill an old lady. (lines 10 and 11) Again return to our full shot . . . script indicates Kovacs and Edie *in*. Edie sings:

And when he'd ride in the afternoon,
I'd follow with a hickory broom,
The pony being rather shy
When bitten by the blue-tail fly

Again for lines 16, 17, 18, closer view of fly and buttermilk. Script indicates Kovacs and Edie out. After last line the fly is rather winded, returns to his chair puffing a bit, valet comes out with a glass of scotch and ice, and squirts seltzer in it. Music is stopped during this. Fly gestures and Edie sings lines 19 and 20. She sings this while we are still on fly. A little on the *mal de mer* side from the thought of this woman swallowing a spider.

Note: on the full shot, they must always be the same size as we cannot change size of faces.

Return to the full shot for lines 21, 22, 23, 24. Script Edie and Ernie in. These lines (music and Edie be notified) will be done rather classically with sweeping violins and cowboy outfit will abruptly change to evening dress for Edie and tails for Ernie. Bass will change to violin for Kovacs and guitar will become harp for Adams, just on these lines 21, 22, 23, and 24.

Kovacs and Adams out.

Then return to our fly shot ... who is just finishing his highball . . . He is a little bagged now. And we have some little bubbles or something above him to show his drunkenness and indications around the eyes and nose.

Edie and Ernie sing off camera,
Flies in the buttermilk (lines 25, 26, and 27 . . . in the middle of line 25 fly tries to get up, can't make it. Manages to get over to pitcher on line 26 and finally does a fairly good though drunken time step. Obviously because he can not climb into the pitcher with the buttermilk and goober peas. We will change lines to original for lines 29, 30. Instead of cheese and rye, it will be "*I know an old lady who swallowed a horse*" (while on c.u. of fly) who immediately says "*Ridiculous*" and the line follows that is "*She's dead, of course.*" After this line wide shot with all three doing a time step for about four fast bars as a finish to music. They do a typical vaudevillian finish. The stamp to the right foot and the right hand out to acknowledge applause, and here we go out of film . . . .

Text of memo sent to staff for third Special, taped May 28, 1961, aired May 15, 1961.

The following is going to be either the downfall of us technically or at least mentally.

Here are the instructions for the construction and various little activities regarding what we will call the "Jealousy" bit. We're going to shoot it in three sections. This is to offset using a million extra people and also to make it somewhat easier as this is a particularly difficult thing to handle technically where there are going to be many willing hands fumbling the shit out of this one including my own. Look at it this way: This is the last one of the four and if everything goes well, I may turn down the proposition to do twelve (wouldn't that be a kick in the ass!) next year.

I am attaching to this the drawings:

Drawing No. 1: You will see a water cooler upstage. This is very deceptive. It is more than a water cooler. In front of the water cooler is a typewriter on a stand. In back of the water cooler is a clock. On top of the clock is a little black bird. (This is the little rubber black bird that works with the rubber ball. I'll show it to you and I think we should get a million of them in case they go bad. I think 6 really ought to do it. See, I remembered the budget.)

The table holding the typewriter must be high enough so that the roller on the typewriter is a couple of inches above the metal part of the water cooler. In other words, a couple of inches on to the lower part of the glass. The typewriter must have four keys that can work by remote control. They will work — one, two, three . . . one, two, three . . . one, two, three, four. (I believe that's the correct order . . . the fourth key is only used once at the end.) The others go in succession — left to right, right to left, left to right and the fourth one. The water cooler must have two separate working effects that can be worked completely under control. Water spout must shoot out water in spurts, and we must have an air hose that can start bubbles at the bottom of the glass water cooler, either in short spurts or long streams.

The clock is a fairly fast-moving clock and must move completely in time with the music. I think you'll find that the pendulum on the clock swings about two times to the second. The little bird will be worked by a rubber ball . . . this is all up against the wall as you can see from the drawing. The clock should be located on the wall so that the lower rim of the clock is about an inch below the top rim of the glass cooler. On the center of the clock, at the top, is where the little black bird is located. Use a medium gray wall on this set.

To the stage left of this is a filing cabinet. There are three drawers, medium, and the bottom drawer should be larger. These drawers must be able to be worked individually from the back as you would slide a trombone. Fake it with a little paper inside as though they were filled. The bottom drawer could be empty, but paint it black inside. The bottom drawer must also work like a slide trombone and at the end will slide out something like six feet, or eight even, if we can.

To the left of this is a radiator. At the end of the bit, the very end of the bit, we must have a good spout of steam come out of the valve. The valve should be located stage *right* of the radiator. In other words, it is on the stage right side of the radiator which locates it between the filing cabinet and the radiator. To stage left of the radiator is a switchboard. And if you think you had trouble, wait till you read this. We should get a switchboard with approximately 6 rows of lights, *if possible.* These must be able to work as we want them. The main effect will be starting at the top left row and going all the way to the end of that row, and starting at right of the second row and going all the way to the left of the second row, starting at the left of the third row and going all the way to the right of the third row, starting at the right of the fourth and going to the left of the fifth row and so forth. In other words, it comes down snakelike . . . a kind of backward "s" design all the way down. The keys that are flipped on this board should be painted white so that they can be seen and I would like to be able to work them either individually and/or as a group (manually). There should be four of the line connectors (the long cords that are stuck into the board). They should be painted a light gray color, and they must be made to flip back and forth. I will describe that a little better. If they are slightly bowed and can be made to sway in unison, that is the effect we want. If it also can be added that we can push them out from the back at the end, that would be helpful. The desk, which is stage right of the water cooler (disregarding the top of the desk which is really complicated), must have the drawers in this manner: facing the desk and starting at the lower left side, I would like the drawers to go open in succession, bottom left first, next one next, top left next, center top next, right top next, and the other two in that same order, then reverse and have them close in the same order. The top of the desk is where we get complicated.

And now we can see Drawing No. 2 for this one: I do not think that the width of the desk should be too much, but I would suggest no less than three feet. Facing the desk on the lower left hand corner is a large old fashioned fountain pen lying on a large white sheet of paper, preferably three or four sheets of paper — blank. In time to the music, this pen must drop gobs of ink out of the point. The phone, which will be located directly in back of the pen, must have the dial work briefly. Only one full turn will be needed in synchronization to the music in short movements, a kind of synocopated beat. The ear-piece and talking-piece of the phone must be made to rock back and forth in time to the music while remaining on the cradle. It raises on one end, drops, raises on the other end, and drops. This also must be completely controlled manually. To the right of the phone is an old-fashioned pencil sharpener, with the hole facing us. I would like a little electric motor to turn the handle which will be at the back, but the handle should be big enough so that we can still see the end of the handle going around in the back. Directly in back of this is the water carafe with a large Thermos-type cork stuck on top. This must be made to raise and lower on musical cue. I would suggest that the cork be about 4 inches long so that we can push it up as high as that much and lower it again. (Again facing the desk.) To the right of this carafe are four water glasses. These must be able to be tapped from the bottom so that they will move, visibly. On the lower right end of the desk is a desk spindle which is possibly the most interesting device on the desk. This should have three sheets of paper approximately 5 by 7 with some scribbling on it attached at equal distance places on the spindle. I would like this to work in this manner that the spindle can be pulled into the desk, pushed up again and the pieces of paper will resume their original position. The spindle should be about eight inches high but also capable of going another twelve inches up for effect. At limbo, I would like ten paper clips on what appears to be a tray. The effect that I would like on this tray (and remember it is at limbo) is for us to draw a magnet beneath the tray causing the ten paper clips to pile up at the end, but they must pile up individually. I would humbly suggest that a small series of ridges such as a folded piece of heavy paper laid out with the paper clips placed on the side of the ridge so that when the magnet is drawn from the right to the left, the paper clips will not go over the ridge. However, they will go off at the other end. This is much in the manner of some shallow steps. Picturing this as a shallow stairway with the paper clips in each one and a magnet drawn from the top of the stairs to the bottom, the paper clips could not physically go up the steps to meet the magnet, but as the magnet passes underneath, it would gather each of the paper clips to pile up on the bottom step. As we are going to shoot this in sections, let us discuss manpower.

In order to save some money on this, we will shoot this in sections rather than as a whole. Therefore, we can have some people double on instruments, as the expression goes. We will need two people working the filing cabinet. At the water cooler the clock can be on a motor but the bird will be operated manually, the typewriter will be operated manually and the water cooler will be operated manually. However, the typewriter will be operated and then we will lift the camera off it, so whoever is operating the typewriter can also work the water cooler. When we are on the bird, that will be operating all by itself. I leave it to you to work this out as best you can. Later, at the water cooler, there is one thing that I forgot to discuss above. There is a paper-cup dispenser beside it. Four times (two times each, each two in close succession to the other) I need a whole zing of papercups to shoot out. They can come out disjointed, or they can come out in one long stream, it doesn't matter . . . if it's easier in one long stream we'll do it that way. The paper clips, of course, we'll need one man to operate, and if it will help any, we can shoot that as an insert. The switchboard we'll need one person operating the lights, one person operating the keys. The person operating the keys can also operate the cables. The desk in this first sequence, we'll need the operation of the seven drawers opening in that sweeping "U" turn, and then closing in that sweeping "U" turn. And that is our problem. I would like Bobby Hughes to work the water cooler, certainly, the bird, and the typewriter. The stuff that is on top of the desk will be shot separately so that the same people operating that can operate the top of the desk. On top of the desk I would like Bobby to work the fountain pen and the glasses and anything else that he can operate from there. The pencil sharpener can be worked on an electric switch and the bottom turned on to have the handle revolve when we need it and will not require attention. Your big problem, obviously, will be in grouping this stuff so that it can be operated and still have those drawers operating. Consequently, someone obviously underneath the desk. I suggest a fake backing for the knee hole section so that someone can actually sit there and work these things. If it is necessary to group them more towards the center than I have indicated, we can do that.

I don't know how the hell you're going to get this done by Sunday, but "rots of ruck."

— *Ernie (with love)*

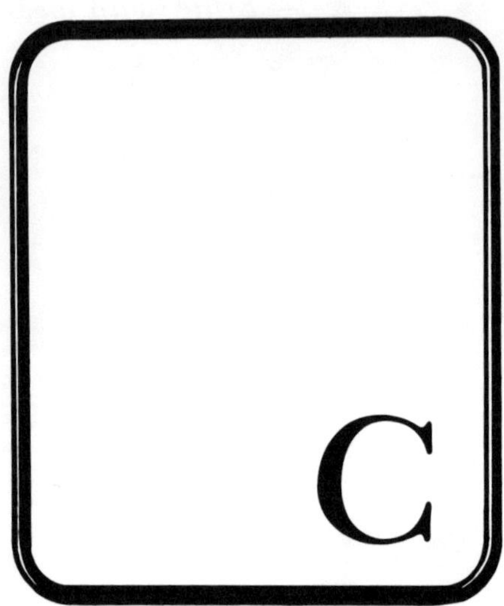

December 30, 1952 . . . Prop List

1 Cigar with long thread
2 Wooden watch with long thread
3 Cap gun
4 Bath robe
5 Hat (battered)
6 Title cards: Wolfgang Sauerbraten on the Air (luminous paint)
7 Props for Pfffif (deodorant) — very large hot-water bottle and large economy-size bottle (Trig)
8 Shirt with painted arm holes (Andy)
9 Wolfgang Sauerbraten (Andy)
10 Single chime for time signal, small mallet
11 Bottle labeled: Raus mit (Trig)

12 Piece of cloth to polish piano
13 Cue cards for Sauerbraten bit
14 15 records for the Sauerbraten bit
15 Blonde pig-tailed wig for Edie
16 German outfit
17 Postal card. On address side: To Wolfgang Sauerbraten CBS TV, N.Y.
18 Names of Hungarian pieces from Hatrak for clearance
19 5 complete sets of broken dishes and cups
20 2 title cards: Already drawn (Trig, Lady Flatbush, Roger the Lodger)
21 Sep. script large print of Roger the Lodger offer on desk for Kovacs
22 Super of 43 cents (for Roger the Lodger)
1 roll of car tape
Corset stays
Pound of window putty on dish
One doz. frankfurters, linked
Candelabra
Marshmallow sundae in dish
Table cloth
23 Four local phone numbers
Four out-of-town phone numbers
Same as above written out for Kovacs to be read
24 Sheets for tonsorial barber-shop quartet song
25 Towel, hot, and shaving cream and brush for lather (Rise) cup, razor
26 Costumes for two barbers and two customers
27 The Hatrak Barber Show with winter garb on it: old-fashioned winter coat and garb, Sauerbraten's coat can be used, and a couple of derbys
28 Pic of Dad Dovetonsils
29 Costume for Percy, cigarette holder and cigarette
30 Script large type of Trig Lund for razor bit

31 3 cards: Look Sharp, Feel Sharp, *Cut Yourself*
32 Baseball outfit for Kovacs
33 Dope wig
34 7 or 8 pieces of metal about 3″ long
35 Safety razor
36 Box of bandaids for Ed Hatrak
37 *Note: Russ must be notified for all sound effects to be used Tuesday night*
38 Diver's helmet
Large anchor
Tank with water and hose (these are for super on Where do you Worka, John?)
39 Cards, title for Where do you Worka, John? prize book, and desk sign
40 Foop bottle (See Trig: filled with powder)
41 Large-type script for Trigger
42 Script for K, Where do you Worka, John?
43 Measles card and filter, and cut-out figure (see Trigger)

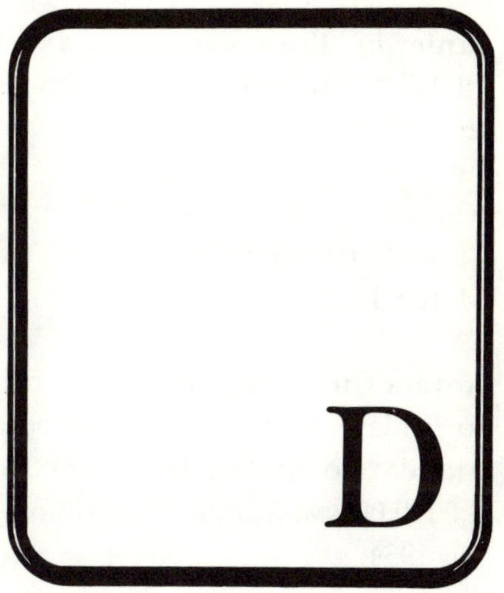

TV SHOWS

Ernie Kovacs in Philadelphia, Pa., from March 20, 1950, to April 18, 1952, on WPTZ (local and NBC).

Deadline for Dinner Local, sponsored cooking show, 2:00 2:30 PM, twice a week, March 20, 1950, to April 18, 1952.

Three to Get Ready Local, sponsored variety show, Monday to Friday, November 27, 1950, to March 28, 1952; 7:30 9:00 AM, November 27, 1950, to September 14, 1951; 7:00 9:00 AM, September 17, 1951, to March 28, 1952.

THE ERNIE KOVACS PHILE

It's Time for Ernie NBC TV network variety show, 3:15 3:30 PM, Monday to Friday, May 14, 1951, to June 29, 1951.

Now You're Cooking Local, sponsored cooking show, 2:00 2:30 PM, once a week, May 15 to June 12, 1951; September 18 to October 16, 1951.

Ernie in Kovacsland NBC TV, network variety show, 7:00 7:30 AM, Monday to Friday, July 2 to August 24, 1951 (replaced *Kukla, Fran & Ollie* for vacation).

Kovacs on the Korner NBC TV, network variety show, 11:30 12:00 Noon, Monday to Friday, November, 1951, to March 1952.

Kovacs Unlimited WCBS TV, Local 12:45 1:30 PM, Monday to Friday, April 21 to December 26, 1952; 8:30 9:30 AM, Monday to Friday, December 29, 1952, to July 5, 1953; 8:00 9:00 AM, Monday to Friday, July 8, 1953, to January 15, 1954.

NOTE: While the above show was on the air, another show was inaugurated, namely, the following:

The Ernie Kovacs Show CBS TV network (opposite Milton Berle on NBC TV) 8:00 9:00 PM, Tuesdays, December 30, 1952, to April 14, 1953.

The Ernie Kovacs Show WABC (Dumont TV), Local 11:15 PM 12:15 AM, Monday to Friday, April 12, 1954 to January 7, 1955.
10:30 11:00 PM, Tuesdays and Thursdays, January 11 to February 24, 1955. 10:00 11:00 PM, Tuesdays and Thursdays, March 1 to April 7, 1955.

NOTE: This last one-hour show was called *The Ernie Kovacs Rehearsal*

ABC Radio's Tonight NBC TV Network 11:00 PM to 1:00 AM, Mondays and Tuesdays, November 1956 to January 1957; October 1, 1956, to January 22, 1957.

CBS TV APPEARANCES

April 21, 1952 to January 15, 1954 (8:00 PM): **Kovacs Unlimited** (Local) January 6 to April 14, 1953 (8:00 9:00 PM): **The Ernie Kovacs Show** March 5 to July 2, 1954: **I'll Buy That** (panelist)
June 6, 1955: **Person-to-Person** (guest)
July 21, 1957: **The Ed Sullivan Show**
July 27, 1958: **The Ed Sullivan Show**
September 26, 1957: **Playhouse 90** *"Topaze"* (star)
June 6, 1958: **The Big Record** (General Motors) (guest)
October 19, 1958: **GE Theater** *"The World's Greatest Quarterback"* (Sam Lund)
February 2, 1959: **Westinghouse/Desilu Playhouse** *"Symbol of Authority"* (Arthur Witten)
February 15, 1959: **GE Theater** *"I was a Bloodhound"* (Barney Colby)
April 1, 1960: **Westinghouse/Lucille Ball/Desi Arnaz Show** (guest)
March 8, 1961: **US Steel Hour** "Private Eye, Private Eye"

RADIO

ABC Radio's **Tonight** NBC TV Network 11:00 PM to 1:00 AM Mondays and Tuesdays, November 1956 to January 1957; October 1, 1956, to January 22, 1957.
November 3, 1957: **The Mitch Miller Show**
September 9, 1956: **The Mitch Miller Show**
August 5, 1957: **This Is New York**

APPEARANCES ON NBC TV

March 7 to March 9, 1951: **It's Time for Ernie** (Phila.)

May 14 to June 29, 1951: **Time for Ernie** (Phila.)

July 2 to August 24, 1951: **Ernie in Kovacsland** (Phila.)

September 2, 1951: VIM Electric **Vim Talent Search** (WNBT) (guest panelist)

September 20, 1951: VIM Electric **Quick on the Draw** (WNBT) (guest panelist)

September 30, 1951: VIM Electric **Quick on the Draw** (WNBT) (guest judge)

October 11, 1951: VIM Electric **Quick on the Draw** (WNBT)

January 7, 1951 to March 28, 1952: **Kovacs on the Corner** (Phila.) (features folks who frequent Kovacs's Alley) (network)

April 27, 1955: **Tonight** (Steve Allen host, Kovacs guest)

June 24, 1955: **Tonight** (Steve Allen host, Kovacs guest)

August 29 to September 13, 1955: **Tonight** (substitute for Steve Allen)

December 9, 1955: **Tonight** (guest)

December 12, 1955 to July 27, 1956: **The Ernie Kovacs Show** 10:30 11:00 AM, Monday to Friday

December 7, 1955: **Home** (guest interviewed)

December 9, 1955: **Today** (guest interviewed)

January 15, 1956: **NBC Comedy Hour** (featured guest)

July 1, 1956: **The Steve Allen Show** (guest)

July 2 to September 10, 1956: **The Ernie Kovacs Show** (replacement for Sid Caesar)

September 21, 1956: **It Could Be You** (guest)

September 28, 1956: **Today** (horticulture sketch with Dave Garroway)

October 5, 1956: **The Walter Winchell Show**

October 1, 1956 to January 22, 1957: **Tonight** (Monday and Tuesday nights alternating with Allen's Wednesday and Friday nights)

November 22, 1956: **Parades 1956** Macy's Thanksgiving Parade
December 9, 1956
March 30, 1957
May 12, 1957
June 9, 1957
Wide Wide World
(film commercial
with Edie Adams
for GM)
December 22, 1956: **Saturday Color Carnival** "The Sonja Henie Ice Spectacular"
February 23, 1956: **The Perry Como Show**
January 19, 1957: **Saturday Color Carnival — The Ernie Kovacs Show** "Silent Show" (half-hour replacement for Jerry Lewis)
February 15, 1957: **Tonight! America After Dark**(via switch to Hawaiian Room, Lexington Hotel, N.Y.)
February 16, 1957: **Saturday Color Carnival** TV Emmy Show (performer)
March 16, 1957: **Saturday Color Carnival** Academy Awards
March 31, 1957: **Wide Wide World** "Spring Jubilee" from Beverly Hills Hotel (remote pickup of fashion show)
May 27, 1957: **Producer's Showcase — Festival of Magic** (emcee)
May 20, 1957: **Truth or Consequences** (guest participant)
July 26, 1957: **Tonight! America After Dark** (interview with Edie in N.Y.C. apartment)
August 20, 1957: **Tex and Jinx Show** (guest interview)
November 10, 1957: **Wide, Wide World** "The Fabulous Infant" (silent comedy bit on kinescope and appears *live*; talks about career in TV)
October 5, 1957: Max Factor — **The Polly Bergen Show** (guest)

October 23, 1957: **Today** (interview on book *Zoomar*)
October 26, 1957: **The Perry Como Show** (guest)
October 29, 1957: **Bride & Groom** (special guest)
November 24, 1957: **The Dinah Shore Chevy Show** (guest)
December 20, 1957: **Truth or Consequences** (guest)
December 31, 1957: **George Gobel Show** (guest)
June 18, 1958: **Today** Film (5:05) of K getting haircut for movie role
October 16, 1958: Ford Motor — **The Ford Show** Tennessee Ernie Ford (guest)
February 15, 1959: **The Eddie Fisher Show**
April 6, 1959: **Oscar Show**
May 22, 1959: **Kovacs on Music**
October 6, 1959: **Ford Motor Startime** *"The Wonderful World of Entertainment"* (guest)
December 11, 1959: Buick — **Bob Hope Buick Show** (guest)
April 11, 1960: Goodyear Tire and Rubber Company — **Goodyear Theater** (stars as Maximilian Krob in Durrenmatt's *Author at Work*)
February 22, 1961: **Here's Hollywood**
May 22, 1962: **14th Annual Emmy Awards** Tape of scene from one of specials and tape of scene from "Laughter USA"

APPEARANCES ON RADIO

July 22 to July 25, 1957: **Nightline** Tape-narrated series called "Hungarian White Paper." A study of this important document quoting from essential texts and using actual NBC News broadcasts of that period (Hungarian revolt).
March 31, 1958: **Groucho Marx** (guest)

THE FILMS OF ERNIE KOVACS

TITLE	RELEASE DATE	DIRECTOR	ACTORS
Operation Madball (Columbia)	1957	Richard Quine	Jack Lemmon, Mickey Rooney, Arthur O'Connell, Kathryn Grant, Ernie Kovacs
Bell, Book and Candle (Columbia)	1959	Richard Quine	James Stewart, Kim Novak, Jack Lemmon, Ernie Kovacs, Hermione Gingold, Janice Rule, Elsa Lancaster
It Happened to Jane (Columbia)	1959	Richard Quine	Doris Day, Jack Lemmon, Ernie Kovacs
Our Man in Havana (Columbia)	1960	Carol Reed	Alec Guinness, Burl Ives, Maureen O'Hara, Noel Coward, Sir Ralph Richardson, Jo Morrow, Ernie Kovacs
Strangers When We Meet (Columbia)	1960	Richard Quine	Kirk Douglas, Kim Novak, Barbara Rush, Ernie Kovacs
Wake Me When It's Over (Fox)	1960	Mervyn Leroy	Jack Warden, Dick Shawn, Margot Moore, Ernie Kovacs
North to Alaska (Fox)	1960	Henry Hathaway	John Wayne, Fabian, Stewart Granger, Capucine, Mickey Schaghnessy, Ernie Kovacs
Five Golden Hours (Columbia)	1961	Mario Zampi	Cyd Charisse, George Saunders, Ernie Kovacs
Sail a Crooked Ship (Columbia)	1962	Irving Brecher	Robert Wagner, Delores Hart, Carolyn Jones Ernie Kovacs

Acknowledgements

I would like to thank the people who aided me in the creation of *The Ernie Kovacs Phile* (formerly *Nothing in Moderation*). Without them it would have only remained an idea.

In Trenton, New Jersey: The staff of the *Trentonian* who welcomed me with open arms, gave me a desk, and allowed me to peruse the morgue at my leisure; Ed Hatrak and Edna Vine for the cake, coffee, and interviews; Sam Jacobs; J. Walter Schnorbus; Albert Mathesius for bending the rules a bit; W. Coe McKeeby for undertaking more than a couple of wild goose chases through the N.J. State court system; Barbara Schaff and John A. Schaff, my sister and brother-in-law for their hospitality on cold winter nights.

In Philadelphia, Pennsylvania: Ms. Geri Duclow, curator of the Theatre Collection of the Free Library of Philadelphia, for her invaluable aid in tracking down stray articles; Mr. Harry Harris from the *Philadelphia Inquirer* for some of his old Kovacs columns.

In New York City, New York: I thank Harriet Van Horne, a truly elegant lady for her reflections; Marc Connelly; Ken McCormick, Editor-in-Chief at Doubleday and Company who provided me with invaluable letters from his files; Vincent Sardi, Jr., and Martyn, the headwaiter at Sardi's, for the lunch and the chat; Rex Lardiner who I hope likes this book; Tom Loeb at CBS for the leads; Shirley Mellner; Jack Mogulescu for his musings on the Olive and Dutch Masters for the loan of his clipping book; to Abu Ben Gaiti and "Rizz" at Channel 5; to the Lincoln Center Library of the Performing Arts Theatrical Collection, invaluable for research in theater and television.

In Los Angeles, California: The Trustees of the University of California at Los Angeles for their permission to quote material from the Kovacs Special Collection; James V. Mink, Director of manuscripts; Hilda Bohem, Director of Public Services who cheerfully responded to my queries and helped me preserve Ernie's records with good folders 'borrowed' from the Music department; and Miles Knudsen, Library Assistant for being there when I occasionally went amok.

I owe my thanks as well to Marvin Moss for the good leads and his candor; to Jack Lemmon for his time and thoughts; to the crews at ABC who gave unstintingly of their energy; to Bob Kemp for his photos; to Bob Haley for the beers; to Bobby Hughes for the script; to Gene Lukowsky; in the 'front office': Edd Henry from Universal, Milt Hoffman, Marianne Hooper from NBC, Joe Behar, Perry Cross, and of course my favorite maverick Barry Shear.

To Edie Adams, a special debt of gratitude for her patience and for her foresight in providing, not only myself, but future students of comedy in general, and Ernie in particular, the Special Collections Department Graduate Library at UCLA with his papers, scripts and assorted memorabilia.

Thanks to Katy Hunt for the space in her livingroom at Honey Drive, Laurel Canyon, where I worked and transcribed for the summer of 1973; to Tandy Brodey, my good friend, who got me the space, gave me her companionship and the use of her car; to all the other inhabitants of Honey Drive who helped make that time magical in my life.

I also owe a special debt of gratitude to Andy McKay, a prince among men, who not only provided me with a solid chronology of Ernie's early years of Philadelphia and New York television but who also introduced me to

Mary Lou Cassidy whose insightful and informative chapter from her uncompleted Masters dissertation on Ernie served as the basis for my own third chapter. I wish to thank her for her Texas encouragement in the face of despair and her correspondence which answered many other questions.

Lastly, I'm grateful to Jeffrey Steinberg, publisher, and Esther Mitgang, my patient and careful editor from Bolder Books for their solid wisdom.

In the final analysis it was the spirit of Ernie which made all my interviews and discussions so rewarding, which motivated me to pursue this project to its inevitable conclusion. I hope I've pleased him.

New York City, 1978

DAVID G. WALLEY

Through a bizarre set of circumstances involving, among other things, an Oreo cookie, Walley became a critic for *Jazz and Pop Magazine* and *The East Village Other*. His articles also appeared in *Rock Magazine*, *University Review*, *Zygote Magazine*, *The New York Ace* and *The New York Herald*. In 1972 Walley broke out of the underground with his nationally acclaimed biography of Frank Zappa entitled *NO COMMERCIAL POTENTIAL: THE SAGA OF FRANK ZAPPA AND THE MOTHERS OF INVENTION* published by E.P. Dutton. Mr. Walley is currently working on a rock n' roll murder mystery.